Rocket Way

OrangeBooks Publication

Smriti Nagar, Bhilai, Chhattisgarh - 490020

Website: **www.orangebooks.in**

© Copyright, 2023, Author

All rights reserved. No part of this book may be reproduced, stored in a retrieval system, or transmitted, in any form by any means, electronic, mechanical, magnetic, optical, chemical, manual, photocopying, recording or otherwise, without the prior written consent of its writer.

First Edition, 2023

ISBN: 978-93-5621-298-5

ROCKET WAY

19 titles to make your small business "HAPPY"

RANJITH

OrangeBooks Publication
www.orangebooks.in

Journey Begins Here

"Who deserves all the happiness in this world?" a disciple once asked Thiruvalluvar (a renowned saint-poet who wrote Tamil's all-time epic "Thirukkural").

"Happiness is only deserved by a mother whose child becomes renowned, and she cries with happiness," Thiruvalluvar answered.

A few years back, I came across this mystical statement while reading a book. It has had my attention for quite some time. I've always been captivated by the wisdom of our ancient sages. They lived and died far more gracefully than we do, and we are in no way comparable to them. They were far more accomplished than we are. It reflects on their works, whether it is philosophy, spirituality, art, war, science, technology, architecture, innovation, sex, business, or economics.

Most of their works are beyond our ability to contemplate in a single lifetime. I have always found inspiration from their lives and writings when trying to make sense of my own existence.

How can a person like Thiruvalluvar make such an unusual claim? I was always perplexed as to why he picked just a mother; why wouldn't a father, sibling, spouse, or anyone else deserve happiness? After sifting through several references and books, I uncovered something I would like to share with you all.

Love; I've come to believe that love is the root of all happiness. Everything great that has transpired here is because of love.

Thus, what exactly is love?

Love is "unconditional," love is "trust", and love is 'forgiveness". Love is never whole if one of these three elements is gone. This was the WOW moment of my life. I just declassified the "love code."

I got a range of responses after sharing this result with my peers. Many of them suggested I should include respect. Respect, I told them, is a secondary emotion. To show respect, we shall look for various qualities in others. Oftentimes, we disrespect people whom we once held in high regard.

One of my friends said he was very happy when he got admission to his dream university. Another one said he was happy when he received his first visa to go abroad. Another person told me his heart was pounding with happiness when his girlfriend finally accepted his proposal. And there were many more suggestions and denials.

Finally, I answered everyone, "Look, it is clear that you were all happy because your desires were fulfilled. It is a temporary state of our mind; it is "joy." It is not "happiness." Happiness is a natural condition. If you feel happiness in certain positions and situations, it will lead to more misery in life. Love is the process, not the result. If you continually seek satisfaction in outcomes, you will never appreciate the process, and hence, you will never be happy.

For some people, happiness is freedom. It is an enjoyable experience for some. For some, it is material possession. For some, it is about gratifying their desires. For some, it is a change in circumstances. We all chase happiness down the wrong path.

When our desires are gratified, we experience a temporary increase in chemical and hormonal production, that's it; it is not happiness. In Sanskrit, "sukha" means lasting happiness within the being. Then how can we be happy if we look for happiness in certain situations?

This equation covers every relationship perfectly. Have you ever wondered why some friendships don't last? Because we are unwilling to forgive others' faults. Why do couples who have been together for a long time eventually separate? It's because trust has been broken. Assess which of these three elements of love is out of balance when you have an issue with someone, whether it is your spouse, parents, friends, co-workers, or employees. To restore harmony and happiness in your relationship, you must strive to build trust, maintain an unconditional attitude, and engage in forgiveness.

You get in fine tune with nature as your love approaches infinity, and you become more miserable when you can't express love and appreciate everything in this world.

If you have pets, you must have experienced this natural condition of "happiness." It is demonstrated in research studies that interaction with animals reduces cortisol and blood pressure. It is because you are genuinely in love with your pet. You have an unconditional relationship with your pet. As a result, it is not only philosophically but also scientifically proven that the root cause of happiness is to be in true love with everything and anything.

Surprisingly, only a mother's love for her child exhibits these three fundamental characteristics of love. Only our mother will stay with us if everyone else deserts us. The only person who always wants her kid to be a winner is the mother. This is why we often say that nothing else in the world can compare to a mother's love.

Perhaps it could be the reason Thiruvalluvar believed that only a mother deserves happiness. What an insightful thought!

We deserve to be happy, only if we are in true love. After all, we are made for love.

As a consequence of this idea, I began my research to find out what makes a small business happy. What qualities does a small business need to improve to become a happy place to work?

I had spent my entire career in small-scale industries, and this idea had always been in the back of my mind. For various reasons, I've witnessed several happy and bad stories throughout my career. I was able to connect all the dots when writing my book.

As a result of my research, I've identified that there are exactly "19 titles" that hinder a small business from getting a happy workplace. Each title is significant in determining the level of happiness. The more evident something is, the more significant it becomes. On the other hand most small-scale companies do not focus on these titles.

Content

Heed Me Here	1
Observation: The Third Eye	8
Training: No Longer An Option	20
Performance: Tipping Point	34
The Art of Connection: Communication	52
Recruitment And Beyond	66
Emotional Intelligence: A Superpower	78
Motivation: Pushes to The Extreme	95
Kaizen: Daily Navigator Tool	108
Time Management: The Most Sensible Tool	120
Thinking In Design: World in A New Light	133
Thinking In Systems: We Are Interdependent	147
Thinking In First Principle: From the Source	156
Guidance: Standing At The Front	163
Positive Psychology: Art of Living	179
Willpower: Miracle	195
Productivity: A Mistake Proof Tool	204
Cost Management: For Better Today and Tomorrow	214
Distraction: Free Pass To Hell	223
Success and Failure: A Philosophy	236
Submission	259

Heed Me Here

While searching for the happiness code, I came across a manufacturing firm. I informed my intention to the manager thereof. He was kind enough to let me interview him. I asked him about the recruiting procedure during our conversation. For their technical department, they hire only diploma holders, not engineering graduates, he said. I was confused. He then explained to me regretfully that the company hired hundreds of engineers, but none of them remained for a longer period or worked very hard. Everyone worked here for a short time. When they got a second offer, everyone took it right away.

On this point, I'd like to disagree with him. Isn't it the company's obligation to make each worker perform at their best? You probably won't be able to hire a good worker, but you can make every worker a high performer. Nobody is perfect, but with the right training and goals, every worker might produce high-quality work.

You hired your first engineer, who failed to do the job; it is not the company's fault. You hired your second engineer, and he failed to give his hundred percent; it was that engineer's mistake. You've hired hundreds of engineers, yet none of them have stayed or worked hard for you, proving the issue is on your end. Instead of changing who you hire, you should change your workplace culture so it attracts the most talented employees on the planet.

According to me, every company has two types of workers: people who lead and make changes, we can call them **"facilitators**,** and people who comply with the instructions and work physically, we can call them **"followers**.**

The facilitators are responsible for company policies, standards, systems, profits, and success. They work mostly with their cognitive capacities. They must have a forward-thinking perspective and a company-first attitude. The facilitator needs to be a creative person. They must have "quality of experience" (more in my title, performance). They should have the capacity to oversee people and resources effectively. Facilitators enable an organization to become the best at what they do.

They help transition a regular company into a great one. Facilitators need to be very confident in every situation. To be a facilitator, one must possess a growth mindset. In the present-day business environment, facilitators must think and act like entrepreneurs.

Facilitators should always be humble in character, intelligent in action, innovative in thinking, and optimistic in perspective.

The "follower" types are more physically active workers. They are the producers in a company and must adopt a follower-oriented mindset. They must follow the schedule and procedures set forth by the facilitators. If they are unable to perform a system's functions efficiently, they constitute the main bottleneck.

Followers need a quantity of experience in their relevant domain. The more relevant their experience, the better it will serve the organization (the time required to perform a task decreases as a worker gains experience). Their contribution is measured in lead time, which is a metric that indexes the time taken to finish a product or service from start to delivery. An ideal follower's responsibility is to maintain operational efficiency.

Many of us believe that the followers are the source of all troubles because they are the most active workers. But this idea needs to be corrected. Facilitators are the root cause of every problem. Facilitators are the root cause of the problem; If you read any history or biography, you won't find a single company that failed because of its followers (workers). The followers can't do anything magical if the facilitators can't solve all the problems or make good decisions.

Facilitators have the habit of fire their followers if something goes wrong. Instead of berating followers for their mistakes, try helping them learn from their experiences and move on with confidence. It is unfair to blame the followers if facilitators fail to provide a platform for them to perform at their full potential.

To achieve the best results, facilitators and followers must work together seamlessly. The greater the disparity between them in knowledge, experience, and attitude, the greater the company's challenges. In most successful businesses, both facilitators and followers operate at their peak levels of efficiency.

The majority of small businesses fail to specify clearly what facilitators and followers are expected to do in their jobs. Because of this, facilitators work as followers. Furthermore, many small businesses regard followers as facilitators. Imagine a company full of followers. Is there anything good that can be expected?

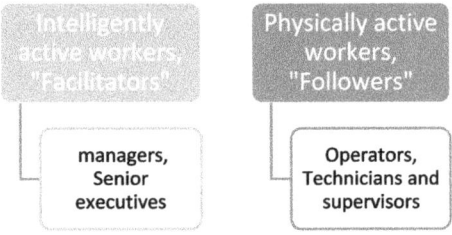

The "facilitators" need to be hired slowly and fired fast because they are the change-makers in your company. The growth is completely dependent on them. The business would continue to suffer if the facilitators failed to fix the challenges.

The "followers" must be hired quickly and fired slowly. The longer an employee remains with a company, the greater their understanding of the process and customer requirements. They needed a little instruction about anything if they stayed longer. It will save a great deal of time and effort and benefit the organization in the long run. If you disregard your followers, you will have to devote more time to interviews, orientation training, communication, and monitoring. It is a non-value-added activity and slows down operational efficiency.

Non-value-added activity has a snowball effect that will cause you to lose all your passive and active customers.

For example, assume you own a small toy manufacturing company. Your business has ten workers (followers) and one manager (facilitator). You produce hundred toys every month with your ten employees.

Let's say you started your company in the year 2000, and your goal is to have a profitable company in five years. Suppose your facilitator (manager) is incapable of analysing the data, optimizing the processes, improving the system, setting standards, resolving individual problems, adopting the change, inspiring your team, and failing to focus on customer satisfaction. In that case, your workers (followers) will do their job the same way they were doing it exactly the year when you started the company. Nothing has changed over the years.

However, everything will change over time. All of your direct and indirect costs will go up every year. You need to spend more money compared to last year on your operations to produce the same quantity of toys. You may end up with more liability in your business over time.

It is possible that several new companies may start production units similar to yours. Over time, the level of competition will rise. When the process is repetitive, workers will get bored and frequently quit your company. It will increase the attrition rate. A higher attrition rate means you have no long-term employees who can contribute to improvement activities. Everyone is new and fresh to the company. No worker in your company can understand your expectations and requirements.

You will now have many bottlenecks and blind spots that you have ignored over the years, and because of that, your production output will be lower than in the previous years. You had to compromise on your commitment, quality, delivery, and productivity. Profit margins will go down year after year. All your good employees will move to a better company. You will continuously blame your employees for all your failures, and finally, you will have to close your business with a huge debt on your shoulders.

Today, making mistakes is a choice. All companies have made countless mistakes in the past. If you can learn from and avoid mistakes other companies did before, you can save a lot of money, time, and effort. A person is called a genius when they learn from others and take the necessary actions to prepare for the future.

A business will grow in three ways: with the help of people; with the help of a system; and with the help of money. As I mentioned, the facilitators will help you grow your business to another level if they are too smart to resolve any problems. With the help of a system, the followers help your business grow. For the best results, it is important to maintain a good relationship between both types of workers. If these two types of employees can't work well together, the business will be stuck in the middle. And finally, the investment. It is not always realistic to have a large amount of capital to invest in a small business setup.

I designed this book to be easy to read and understand. It is not required to read the book page by page; instead, read the book title by title. Each of these nineteen titles carries a nugget of curated knowledge that may help you think afresh. You can utilize the ideas in this book to upgrade yourself and your organization. Writing these "19 titles" in such a small volume was incredibly challenging. Each title deserves to become a stand-alone book.

Most of the books are written by either experts or famous people, but I am neither. This book provides information from the perspective of an insider, not that of a consultant. A consultant will teach you in an academic way, with a lot of rules and laws laid with experience. Not the wisdom of a teacher but rather the observations of a student - that's what you'll find in this book. Therefore, this may be more useful in making changes within you.

I have no doubt that all of these "19 titles" will make you and your small business happier.

The contents of this book are open to critique, and I'd like to hear why you're dissatisfied.

This book was written with the belief that a happy person will constantly seek to make others happy.

Let me wish you a wonderful ride!!!!!!

Observation: The Third Eye

———•———

As we observe more, we absorb more, similar to how a sponge absorbs water. This ability fosters insight. Being insightful allows us to see and understand things that others often miss.

All of us were able to get through the recent pandemic, Corona. We've been working together for more than two years to fight the invisible virus that came from nowhere. It shattered the world economy, pushed many people into starvation and poverty, shut down many businesses, and broke up millions of families and their dreams. During this time, though, we all learned the significance of hygiene in our daily lives. Now we all know how crucial it is to wear a mask, be vaccinated on time, and wash our hands to prevent the spread of the virus.

But there is an incredible story behind modern-day hygiene practices. Ignaz Semmelweis, a 19th-century Hungarian doctor, was known to have found that treating a patient with dirty hands could kill the patient. In 1847, he proposed the idea of a basic hygiene method to stop the deaths of new moms in his hospital from an unidentified illness.

He was working as an obstetrician at the Vienna General Hospital. He had witnessed a high mortality rate among new moms in the hospital, which greatly upset him. More than fifteen percent of new moms brought to the hospital were succumbing to an inexplicable illness known as "childbed fever." Nonetheless, nobody knows what caused these sudden and unexpected fatalities.

He observed surgeons dissecting diseased bodies with their bare hands and delivering babies with the same contaminated hands. In those days, the science of bacteria was not well recognized. He presumed that the autopsy physicians had some sort of indestructible particle in their hands after conducting an autopsy. Following this observation, he mandated everyone entering the labour room wash their hands in a chlorinated lime solution.

After trying to persuade the doctors and staff for a long time, he finally saw the result. Within a few months, the maternal mortality rate dropped to 1%. No one seemed to believe that a doctor was responsible for killing the patients.

No one believed that hand-washing with a chlorinated lime solution could have prevented the deaths of many new moms. His observational abilities, though, were sufficient to discern what was wrong. His findings were fundamental but neglected by all the doctors and staff.

Despite this proof, the majority of the medical communities rejected his theories. Years after his death, in the 19th century, the germ theory of the disease was finally accepted, which confirmed his findings were accurate. He paid close attention to the process, and he was able to find answers that others couldn't.

About 2500 years ago, Aristotle declared the shape of the earth was round. Back then, the consensus was that the earth was a flat object. He came up with the idea of spherical earth based on real evidence. He discovered it after careful observation. He had no tools, such as a telescope, to help him gather evidence.

He observed the ship was no longer visible to him by the time it reached the horizon. If the earth were flat, it wouldn't be possible. During a lunar eclipse, he observed, the earth casts a round shadow on the moon. Different constellations could be seen at different latitudes, which would not be possible if the earth were flat.

He was successful in connecting all the possible dots to substantiate his assertions.

Galileo once said, "I have never met a man so ignorant that I couldn't learn something from him". That is how we found the secret of everything. We learned about photosynthesis by observing the leaves. We observed the sky and learned about the atmosphere and cosmos. Without the ability to observe, we won't be able to come up with new ideas.

Thinking about something new is challenging for our brain and intellect to figure out what it is. Through observation, we will be able to form more in-depth, inductive arguments. It induces our critical thinking capacities to the limit. We're called "critical thinkers" when we know how to ask the right questions at the right time. Without asking the right questions, we will never be able to get answers to our claims and arguments.

Whenever we have so much information, some of them will be false or exaggerated. It distorts our critical thinking skills. We should always verify how trustworthy those sources of information are. Today, we learn more from WhatsApp and Facebook, which is a shame. We constantly rely on secondary information.

With the help of critical thinking skills, it is possible to notice even the smallest details. It is necessary to come up with a proper answer from your observation; otherwise, others will question and disbelieve your claims.

Information is now synonymous with Google in an internet-dominated world. If Google can answer everything, there is no need for any other institution in this world. Nevertheless, if you only listen to what you want to hear, you will only get information that supports your beliefs. This information will render all of your decisions less effective.

Observation is the science of reasoning. In the fields of psychology, education, neuroscience, philosophy, and artificial intelligence, reasoning is used to stimulate thought. The number of answers you have is not so significant, but the number of questions you ask will help you improve your reasoning abilities. The purpose of observation is not to cast more uncertainty on a situation but rather to shed light on it. The more you observe, the more data you acquire, which you can use to expand your business.

Observation: The Third Eye

When we pay attention to the world around us, our imaginations grow. It is possible to define imagination as our sixth sense.

Undoubtedly, most creative people who have ever lived here have harnessed the power of observation. We couldn't have developed our imaginative capacities without the practice of observation. It pushes us to think beyond logic. In his most renowned poem, "Meghaduta," Mahakavi Kalidasa describes the anguish of a Yaksha (Yakshas are the divine attendants of the god of wealth, King Kubera) who was separated from his wife.

Yaksha was so preoccupied with his wife that he neglected to execute his duties. Out of anger, Kubera sentenced him to one year in prison in Ramagiri, central India. He sorely missed his wife, but he was helpless to do anything about it. He was tired and stressed alone in prison. He desperately wanted to be with his wife. That, however, he knew it was not going to happen in one year.

One day, depressed Yaksha chose a cloud to deliver a message to his wife in Alagapuri, a village in the Himalayas. In Kalidasa's imagination, the cloud resembled an elephant. Not only did he convince the cloud to convey his message, but he also instructed the cloud on the route it should take, where to rest, what to look for, when to move swiftly and when to go slowly, when to approach Alagapuri, and how to identify his wife.

How can someone imagine a cloud as an elephant? How is it possible for a cloud to deliver a message? Without imagination, nothing like this kind will ever be created. The reader did enjoy not only the poetry, but also the geography, history, and cultural context as if they were there themselves.

Using our senses effectively is a great way to improve our ability to observe the world around us. Leonardo DaVinci was an extraordinary inventor, engineer, artist, sculptor, and architect, arguably with more ability and intellect than anybody else who lived here. All of his observations and thoughts were meticulously recorded.

Throughout his life, he had written 7,000 pages of observational notes. Every day, he practiced the optimum use of all five of his senses to learn new things. As a means of refining his senses, he actively sought connections between his observations. When we use our senses to the limit, we open the door to the realm of perception. The more we utilize it, the more effective it gets.

For example, according to many studies, if we apply a flower spray before bed, we are more likely to have an excellent sleep and pleasant dreams. There are more than five million receptor cells in our noses. It has a significant impact on our feelings and mental wellness. These scent cells in the nose are connected to the limbic system, the oldest section of the human brain, where emotions, behaviour, and long-term memory are controlled. Most modern research has proved that a good smell significantly affects our emotions, stress, pain, concentration, and memory.

To improve the post-break output rate in Japanese factories, they spray lavender perfume during tea breaks. Also, the vanilla smell enhances creativity, according to research. Apply these ideas to your workplace and observe the changes that ensue.

The concept of biomimicry originates from observing nature. Observing nature and its phenomena enhances our ability to learn and generate new ideas. Unlike the usual industrial approach to design, this method is different.

Scientists have discovered that mimicking the way butterflies' wings absorb sunlight can improve the efficiency of thin-film solar cells. There are many other examples, like wind turbines inspired by whale fins, termite mounds like designs for cooling buildings, bullet trains inspired by the beak of a kingfisher bird, the "V shape" of jets inspired by the birds, and many more. The subject of biomimicry would never have been possible without observation.

Any subject will spark your curiosity as you learn more about it. Be more curious about the world we are in. Like IQ and EQ, the curiosity quotient (CQ) is also very important. If you don't have CQ, you will behave as if you know the answer to everything.

Chandrasekhara Venkata Raman, C.V. Raman, was the first Asian and Indian to receive the noble prize for science in 1930. He won an award for his discovery, known as the Raman effect. Two years after his discovery, he was awarded the Nobel Prize.

It was the general belief that the blue colour of the sky was due to the reflected skylight and the absorption of the light by the suspended matter in the water. Raman had shown that the blue colour of the sea is independent of skylight and absorption. But it is due to molecular diffraction. This finding earned him the Nobel Prize. Many people have noticed the blue tint of the ocean. But nobody prefers observing and questioning it.

It didn't happen by chance. He had a deep interest in nature. He was extremely fascinated by science. At a very young age, he fell in love with physics. He never separated his physics books from his bed, even when he was sick. When he started paying close attention to light, he got fascinated by optics. He worked independently for more than ten years and proved his credibility as a scientist to the outside world.

As you become more observant, you will gain an extra eye to see things that others often miss, an extra flavour that others cannot taste, an extra ear to hear something that others may miss, and an extra sense to perceive things that others can't imagine.

Observation is your second vision that lets you see things beyond what you normally can't.

Reality changes when it is observed. It is known as the "observer effect". The most basic idea in quantum physics is the observer effect. A prominent example is a double-slit experiment. Isaac Newton exemplified the apex of scientific achievement in human history. He described light as a particle. But in the 19th century, a scientist, Thomas Young, ran a classic experiment with light known as the "double-slit experiment", where he passed light through a double slit, two narrow slits separated by a small distance. Instead of light behaving like a particle, it acts like both; a particle and a wave.

The power of observation can contradict any fact or prediction.

Much research has been conducted to study how to improve shop floor worker productivity. One such study is known as the "Hawthorne effect". It refers to the fact that people will modify their behaviour simply because they are being observed. The researchers concluded that workers' productivity was not affected by the changes in their working conditions alone, but rather by the fact that someone was concerned enough about their working conditions.

The workforce has a wealth of knowledge that can be gleaned if management is observant.

Observation is deep (Attention + Focus). By practicing observation, we will become more attentive and concentrated. These observations, which are the most important data, need to be organized, measured, analysed and implemented.

In an interview, billionaire entrepreneur Elon Musk mentioned he spends most of his time inside the Tesla plant. He often sleeps there. He said he could collect real-time data by paying closer attention to the situation whenever he was on the shop floor. In Japanese Lean philosophy, this is known as "Gemba." "Gemba" refers to the place where value is created. Many business owners never go to the Gemba and rely on their favourite employees for information. This results in the formation of an erroneous perception of the situation.

Observation skills may help us better regulate our emotions and develop compassion for others. Positive habits may be formed via observation as well. If you tend to lose your cool easily, it could cause many problems for you. Pay attention to the circumstances that led you to lose your cool. Make a deliberate effort to avoid or redirect the circumstance the next time it occurs. Your anger will subside with time, and you'll learn new ways to deal with it.

It is tough to comprehend the world, but it is easy to comprehend oneself through observation.

The significance of observation in work and our daily lives cannot be avoided. For example, police officers get training in how to observe as a way to improve their ability to conduct investigations. The most critical talent for a police officer is the capacity to gather and analyse readily available information and turn it into evidence. Without paying attention to the specifics, a police officer may be unsure who the victim and the culprit are.

Many of us enjoy reading Sherlock Holmes books because of his superior ability to observe and deduce information. Sherlock Holmes' unique ability to observe crime scenes more closely than any other police officer is the source of his brilliance.

Observational data should include both qualitative and quantitative information. For example, in a machine how much output it gives is quantitative information, whereas who the operator is and what their qualifications and experience are is qualitative information.

"It is easy to miss the obvious" if you don't pay attention. Knowing what your employees are doing and what they are supposed to do, makes all the difference. Often, a single person makes a mistake, and the entire team suffers as a result.

When you observe 10% more than your competition, you perceive several times more primary information. It will significantly help you to outperform your competitors. You're getting free unlimited data from Reliance Jio not because they want to help you become a more knowledgeable person but because they can observe your activities more than their competition to grow their business.

Every element of your business should be subject to change and growth. If we only pay attention to a few measures, we might miss something important. No matter how many obligations we have, we will never be concerned with real-time problems.

When we are just concerned with profit, for instance, we are likely to overlook several crucial details. We disregard many deserving employees when we choose to reward only our favourite ones. Consequently, we ask fundamentally flawed questions and get a disproportionate amount of incorrect information. The cumulative impact of this misinformation will damage a company's focus and reputation.

We always make poor decisions, when we focus only on a few measures. According to research, the majority of our decisions are based on gut feelings, emotions, and little information. We will, however, make better decisions if we can observe these facts in detail. By practicing observation, we can increase our level of awareness. It gives us a greater sense of what's happening around us and helps us make better decisions. A comprehensive grasp of the world and oneself is a state of perfect awareness.

There are only two kinds of events in a workplace: observed and unobserved. It is the best time to switch from being a watcher to an observer if you want to build a happy business.

The only effort we should make is to spend more time going through the entire observation process. Since we assume that waiting time is always dead time, we do not engage in observation.

Training: No Longer An Option

Ramu is a mechanical engineer. He was a top student and graduated with distinction. As soon as he graduated from school, he got a job, which made him very happy. He hoped the time had come to recoup all the money spent on his education.

He was the best student, and everyone, from family to friends, admired him a lot. At work, he naively believed, he would be treated with the same deference. Once he got to work, though, he realized he was utterly clueless. The work environment was very different from what was taught in the classroom. Every day, it got harder and harder for him. His degree held no significance for him now. After three months, he quit his job with no plan for the future.

The greatest challenge he encountered was his inability to address problems in everyday situations. In his 23 years of schooling, he learned only one perspective on solving problems. He had learned nothing in school except how to take tests that were already covered in the textbooks. In a company, there is no textbook of answers that might be studied and applied as-is. He was incapable of teamwork and unable to exert himself. He had poor interpersonal skills. He was afraid of taking responsibility. He could not perceive the company's expectations and requirements. He was unable to handle work pressure and lacked confidence.

Here, training plays an extremely significant role. What if Ramu was given the proper training to be able to work? If you are proud of your business, training is no longer an option.

The purpose of any training is to convert data into practical knowledge. We all have enough theoretical knowledge. In addition to theoretical knowledge, we need something else to perform well. That catalyst is called training.

A well-trained person will always look for opportunities, whereas an untrained person will always quit when the odds are against them. The output of any organization is the sum of its employees' individual efforts. Training helps us perform our daily duties more efficiently, which in turn yields better results.

Everyone has a different set of skills, knowledge, attitude, and performance. The capacity of individuals to absorb information and adjust to circumstances varies. Then, how can we get everyone to have the same goal and work toward it without proper training?

I once asked a senior employee in a production company, "What are you doing here?" "Why are you working here?"

He replied to me very seriously, "Well, I get to work early, I have several meetings a day, I tell my workers what to do, I receive my schedule from my manager, I work as part of a team, I usually work extra hours, when necessary, I deal with our clients, I respond to every email, and so on."

I expected a senior employee's response to be more specific. What if he responded, "I work on three improvement activities", "Our goal is to reduce customer complaints and shop floor mistakes by 50%", or "We are working to reduce the cost of quality control and inspection by 30%", or something like this.

I asked him again, "Are you happy with what you're doing here?" He said, "Yes, I am, and I get paid for it." But if you keep doing the things you mentioned before, I told him, the company won't be happy for you. The functions of your domain and the tasks you do every day are very different. You will never add value to your employer, until you understand this. He was the most experienced worker there, yet he didn't understand what I told him.

Many of the employees I've interviewed have told me this exact thing. But sometimes, employees were too honest, and they said, "Oh, we don't know, we're just busy once we get inside the company."

It is important to know why each person is working for you. Most of the employees lack clarity regarding their job and their role. They hardly know what they must do to achieve a common goal. Everyone is busy with the tasks they do every day. In their daily work, there is almost no value-added proportion. Here I realized how important it is for every small business to provide training, mentoring, and coaching.

With the help of subject matter experts, training will teach you exactly what to do at work to improve productivity, quality, delivery, morale, and customer satisfaction. Training is a compilation of many real-world examples, frameworks, proven methods, assignments, and case studies.

Small companies hesitate to implement training programs because they view training as an expensive and time-consuming process. Here, something valuable is never offered for free. The greater the value, the greater the price. Companies that invest in their workers' training and awareness are the ones that care most about their bottom lines. They are aware that people are the key to growth. Employee motivation, workplace synergy, work quality, and even the quality of a person can be greatly enhanced by good training.

Many problems could arise in your company, making training crucial. If you try to solve every problem on your own, it takes a very long time, and you may not be able to find all the answers. Our lives are short, and trying to know everything on our own won't help us build a happy company. We will lose control over many things if we try to do so. But what if someone had already solved many problems just like yours? The challenges you face will be solved quickly and precisely with their guidance and support.

However, we should know how to choose a better training program. Practically, we require two kinds of training. The first step is to improve ourselves, mostly by learning soft skills. Then there are professional skills, mostly hard skills, which we studied in colleges and other academic institutions to get a job.

Personality development is so important because we don't learn about personality and values in schools or colleges. In school, we were told just to follow the instructions and read the old, irrelevant syllabus. You will be judged based on how well you scored in each grade, rather than how talented you are. Because of our current education, most of us don't have much practical knowledge about values and character building.

Soft skills require most of the training. Soft skills like communication, people skills, work ethic, organizational behaviour, goal setting, customer satisfaction, time management, emotional intelligence, problem-solving, and so on should make up 80% of training. Hard skills like technical knowledge, operational excellence, and quality management should get 20% of the training. Because today, in the information age, it's easy and free to learn any hard skills.

For example, you should expend less time and effort teaching your employees what quality control and its methods (hard skills) are; and you should invest more time in teaching them how to address any quality problems on the spot and how to solve them in their own capacity (soft skill). These are the most effective training strategy to deliver the desired results.

Let me explain how this strategy will benefit you. I often ask senior employees and managers this one question in particular. Let's imagine you bought a brand-new, imported machine to speed up your process. It began malfunctioning after two weeks. You're working on an important project. Your deadline is coming up, and your customer calls you every day to know the progress. You are significantly behind your schedule. What should you do in this situation?

Most of the responses I received were, "I never buy imported machines, I request my customers to wait, I work overtime to compensate for the production, I will try to resolve the issue using locally available resources, I will outsource, and I will make a zoom call to the machine manufacturer to get it ready."

Surprisingly, everyone was focused on the issue and thinking hard about how to solve it after the incident. It is not because of our inability to analyse things, but because of our conditioning. We can create a happy workplace if we modify our approach to the problem. Sadly, we are only able to recognize problems after they have occurred. This is what renders us weaker.

Do you think problems are suddenly coming from another planet to destroy you? No, it was always there unless you had the courage to solve it before it formed a shape.

We live in a very demanding world. If we are afraid of foreseeing problems, our opportunity to rise to the top is over. The best and most productive thing to do is solve it before it actually occurs.

Do this activity. Try to write down all the problems that happened in a day, and by the end of the day, see if there was any way you could have prevented them. Believe me, you can solve 80% of problems before they happen in a small business if you are proactive.

Imagine you teach all of your employees how to solve problems this way. What if every worker in your company began to solve all their problems? Isn't that the best thing that could ever happen to your company?

A well-trained employee will do a good job, and a well-trained manager will lead the company well.

A person who is well-rounded in both soft and hard skills will be a right fit for your company. If you talk to the most successful people, they will say their success is due to their soft skills rather than hard skills. But the majority of our time is spent mastering hard skills. However, they are only helpful in a very small portion of our business or career. You can do well in any job if you spend the time to improve your soft skills.

I know many good mid-level workers don't get promoted to senior positions because they don't have the right skills. They are afraid to take on additional responsibilities. Many good workers are stuck in mid-level jobs even after twenty to twenty-five years of experience, knowing that the mid-level job is the last chance to go up the career ladder.

Suppose you are in a mid-level position. You've been at your job for fifteen years and have decided to apply for a managerial position. Even if you don't have an MBA, you can still be a manager. But you can't be a good manager if you've never learned how to be one. Just having work experience is not enough. Knowing how to handle people, identify and solve more significant problems, have an outsider's perspective, and have good personal ethics are required to become a good leader. Through training, you will learn how to work in different roles. If you don't, there's a good chance you won't do a good job once you are promoted.

The Thiel Fellowship is a training institute founded by billionaire entrepreneur Peter Theil. It is intended for young students under twenty-three years of age who have great vision. They will offer the students a $100,000 grant in two years to drop out of school and work on projects that can change our lives socially, politically, and technologically.

The students from the Thiel Fellowship started more successful ventures than the business schools in a short period of time. They raised more money in venture capital, published more books, developed more mobile apps, created more jobs, and developed more socially committed solutions like bringing clean water to needy people. Ritesh Agarwal, the founder of the OYO hotel chain, was one of Theil's fellowship students.

Due to the outdated curriculum, fees, time commitment, and future benefits, many students rethink their decision to pursue an MBA. Students are looking for these kinds of curated training programs.

Today, we need curated knowledge run by peers and experts in their respective fields, not an outdated syllabus from a university. Usually, experts with lots of different levels of experience in the same field lead the training. When you go to an MBA school, the marketing class is taught by someone who has never worked in marketing or for a marketing company. They teach you what is written in the textbooks.

According to a survey, more than 85% of engineering graduates in India are not qualified to work by industry standards. This 85% of engineers just wanted to get a professional degree to secure a job. Engineering is all about discovering, inventing, and innovating. It can't be explained by a four-year curriculum. Even if we study a single topic for the next forty years, we will still know very little. This type of uninspired workforce compounds the company's challenges. They work to support themselves.

However, everyone who attends training and follows the directions and assignments will develop a more positive attitude toward work and the company.

Furthermore, we must also coach and mentor our employees. Coaching is giving advice and showing the correct path. They need not be experts; they have many tools that can help you achieve what you want. Every employee should receive coaching within the company. Coaches inspire us to maximize our potential. Mentors are those who have achieved a high level of success in their careers. You can heed their guidance on the best course of action. You must have full faith in your mentors throughout the process. Being a mentor is a significant job. Mentors and mentees must get along well with one another. It is a guru-shishya relationship.

We stop learning after college. The industry is changing too fast. Technology changes every two years and is now changing even faster than its current pace. Skill demand is high in the market. Then how is it possible not to train your employees to prepare for the future?

Instead of forcing your employees to attend training, give them a chance to learn themselves. Self-trained workers are more reliable than company-trained workers. There are thousands of online learning courses. Tell your employees to take advantage of these courses.

Everyone in a company has some sort of experience. But being based on experience alone won't help any company grow. We need to figure out how to make these general experiences more meaningful experiences.

For example, you have a lot of work experience but still, have trouble getting the work done on time. If someone can train you how to manage your time, set priorities, focus well, and work as a team, you can solve all your problems on your own. This is how you can turn your experiences into more meaningful ones. Not just for work, but for any experience we have, we need to find a way to transform it into a meaningful experience in order to benefit from it.

Which one do you think is at the top, the employer or the employee? From the customer's point of view, the employer is at the top. But in terms of productivity, performance, growth, and profits, it's all because of employees. Evidently, then, training is essential to the existence of any happy business.

Training: No Longer an Option

Training has been shown to have a variety of positive outcomes, including.

Workers' excuses have gone down by more than 65%.

Decision-making anxiety is reduced by 60%.

Working more than a year without training can lower an employee's morale by up to 60%.

An untrained manager gives unproductive tasks to his employees.

Many employees leave the company because of a lack of career development. As per research, learning and development are the top drivers of employee engagement. The employee will stay long-term in a learning environment.

Transparency, positivity, and communication will improve significantly after every training session.

The number of mistakes will go down significantly. Training will reduce the need for constant supervision.

When employees are trained, they are more likely to make the right decisions and feel more confident.

Giving your employees training and coaching is the only way to get the results you want.

With a positive work environment, employees don't feel like they're putting in a lot of time at the office; instead, they view it as a second home.

A trained employee never hesitates to take on additional responsibilities. A trained employee never resists change.

A good employee has a good EQ and IQ. The best training a company can provide its employees is emotional intelligence. It opens up a new perception of how to live a successful life.

In terms of productivity, a trained employee may perform the work of two or more people.

When your employee communicates better than before, when the team works better than before, when your employee's work ethic is better than before, and when your employee solves problems better than before, your company benefits more than you think.

It took me almost two years to complete this book, but if I had gotten a mentor to help with the process, I could have finished it in one year. Training saves time, and today we don't have the luxury of time.

Not only is it important to provide training, but it is also essential to measure the progress after each training session. Consider that measuring is the second phase of a training program.

Organizational growth lies in individual contributions. The one-man-show model of running a business does not work. Always think you and your employees need to be better and try harder. The day you think you are perfect for running a company is the day when problems will be going to start. Training is the best solution to staying out of it. To grow as an organization, we should realize that both the quality and quantity of contributions from each worker should improve. The quantity of our contribution depends on how hard we work, and the quality of our contribution depends on our talent.

Training: No Longer an Option

This year, on October 13, I heard a very sad news, our military dog, Zoom, had died because of injuries. The news shook my heart. Zoom, a Belgian shepherd, who was two years old and had been a part of the army's 28 army dog unit for the past eight months, was tasked with locating the terrorist's hiding place. During one such operation, terrorists shot him, severely wounding his face and leg; he later succumbed to his injuries. In spite of injuries, he continued his task, which resulted in the neutralization of the terrorists because he was a highly trained dog. What a great life. He deserves the title "hero" because he has done so much for our country.

My point here is, our army cannot arbitrarily select a dog and instruct it to search for terrorists. It needs a lot of training and real-life practice. In the same way, you can't expect more from your employees if they haven't been trained, coached, and mentored. Without training, you cannot expect your workers to meet their obligations to the highest standard.

A machine can produce ten products in a day; it can only produce the same amount even after ten years or maybe less. But if you can nurture the talent of your employees, you will get a million times more benefits over the years.

The advantage of training is it guarantees a balanced workload for everyone. It ensures everyone contributes in the right proportion, which is crucial for any business to achieve higher productivity.

I know a lot of trainers who preach like monks. Employees feel like they're from other planets. In practice, they contribute no value. In a company, the only thing we can control is the process. Therefore, every training should focus on the process rather than the people. When we're in charge of the process, we're in charge of our employees.

In my opinion, cost, training, people, method, and the product are the five pillars of a successful company.

My research suggests that every small business should identify training in at least ten different areas to improve productivity, delivery, quality, and morale.

Performance: Tipping Point

If all you accomplish at work is the bare minimum required, you are at risk of being quickly replaced. But you can excel in your career by applying your skills, effort, interest, and intellect to perform everyday tasks.

The way we live now has a significant impact on how well we function. The fast and hectic pace of city life persuades everyone. But the modern urban lifestyle is neither life-friendly nor performance-friendly. New pubs, clubs, and fast-food restaurants are sprouting up all over the city, while an increasing number of individuals are dissatisfied, unhealthy, uninspired, and hooked.

The number of hospitals has grown, particularly those that treat cancer and other life-threatening disorders. This is because we are essentially shifted away from our genuine and worthy lifestyle, which is specifically designed for our well-being. By chasing enjoyment in life, we inadvertently torment our health. We party so hard on weekends that we can't work throughout the week.

All we need is a steady flow of energy to perform at our best. All energy is constrained in some way, whether it be **mentally, physically, emotionally, or spiritually**. Our energy levels are frequently out of sync because of our lifestyle, which is why we cannot perform adequately and consistently. Let's look at a snapshot of these energies.

The level of **mental energy** is determined by our perspective on life and work. How frequently do you say, "No, I'm not feeling well today," "I hate my boss/company", or "I did not want to do this"? It expresses your current state of mind. It is difficult to do cognitive tasks when we have exhausted our mental energy. If our mental energy is low, we won't be able to pay attention to what is going on right now. We are unable to reach conclusive decisions, recall the procedure and facts, or do any type of analysis. It will impair our ability to think rationally.

Our thoughts produce ideas, which lead to our thinking, which are subsequently translated into actions. We are who we are because of what we do. Absolute awareness of our thoughts will let us act rationally every time. A way to improve our mental awareness is to observe and examine our thoughts and feelings as an outsider.

Do you know why childhood memories are so meaningful to us? Why do we all prefer to remember our school days rather than our adolescent years? We used to live in the present moment when we were kids. We were always joyful and playful. We had a good time. However, as we age, we stop caring about the things that are important in life, such as being in the present moment, being happy with what we have, being curious to learn and explore, and spending time with loved ones.

Being present has considerably more power than we realize. It will allow us to accomplish various tasks more quickly and efficiently than many other methods.

We are incapable of being in the moment because we are perpetually worried. Many of the events we worry about in the future may never happen in our lifetime. So, why are we always worried? We are always anxious about situations that are beyond our control and cannot be predicted. Many of our troubles will disappear when we change our attention to the present moment.

Every one of us carries the burden of our past and worries about the future. If we are burdened with negative experiences, we lose all our efficiency. It is a blessing that, through forgiveness, we can eliminate all our mental burdens. If we can forgive today, our mental energy will be freed up for the most productive tasks. The ability to forgive others may be the key to unlocking our full potential and leading a stress-free life.

Every day we confront our greatest enemy, "fear". Fear of losing, fear of the past, fear of the future, fear of rejection, fear of change, and fear of health. With fear, no one has ever succeeded in this world. We take ourselves too seriously, which is a strange form of selfishness and ego that causes develop fear. Spending time with positive people and your loved ones, and accepting life as it is, is the best way to get rid of unnecessary fear. If you don't conquer your unnecessary fears, you'll always feel angry since fear and anger are interrelated. In the absence of fear, we develop self-confidence.

Meditation elevates our awareness of our thoughts and emotions, thereby improving our mental vitality. We can boost our mental energy by being more aware, doing breathing exercises, and looking at things from a different point of view. Keeping a positive outlook on life is the best way to improve our mental health. Staying organized will allow us to avoid confusion and add greater clarity to the process. Pushing ourselves a bit harder every day eventually results in a strong mind.

This constant feeling of resistance, why is it always there? It is because of so many mental blocks in our way. It is because we experience contradicting circumstances. For instance, you dislike your job but continue doing it every day. You don't like your boss or the company you work for, but you still go to work every day and listen to your boss. This conflicting feeling consistently breeds resistance. When you dislike your work, you produce nothing. Only a person with an open mind, who is a free thinker, and who is courageous can remove all mental barriers.

Stress, anxiety, negative thoughts, unfavourable events and situations, and harmful habits all deplete our mental energy.

Why do we feel it is so hard to control our minds? Because we never try to figure out how our minds work. We never tried to analyse how our mind truly functions. For instance, if you drive a car without learning how to drive, you will crash somewhere. Likewise, if you do not understand your mind, you will never be able to handle it.

Our mind is our master switch. We can govern our lives by channelling our thoughts toward a better direction. Those who master the art of mind control are those who achieve success in life. Always remember you alone are responsible for your current mental state, which may be altered at any moment if you have the confidence to do so.

When we are active, we need a lot of **physical energy**. Sleep, diet, hydration, and exercise are the four factors that have an impact on our health. Maintaining normal blood sugar, pressure, and cholesterol levels is not a sign of good health. To have physical energy means being able to do any task without hesitation.

Sleep is a very scientific process that is often overlooked. To improve their performance, many athletes and well-known sports personalities regularly work with sleep coaches. All great people have definite sleep schedules, especially to help them do their best. If we don't get enough sleep, our brains won't work as well as they should. It leads to a bad mood, inability to focus, micro sleeping, trouble thinking, being unable to process information, difficulty remembering things, and so on.

There are more than forty varieties of sleep disorders, some are common, like insomnia, and some are rare. Our sleep-wake cycle is controlled by the circadian rhythm, which is our body's internal clock. Several studies have shown that our circadian rhythm has a significant impact on our physical and mental health. Building a consistent sleep schedule is the best way to maintain our circadian rhythm.

Many studies have been done on how sleep might help people perform better. In a research study, employees are divided into two groups and given a new subject to work on. Researchers instructed the first set of workers to complete the task by the end of the day and the second set of workers to do it the next day. More than 60% of those who were asked to submit the assignment the next morning delivered excellent results. Learning how to sleep well can completely transform our lives.

The stomach is our best friend. We are what we eat. For example, excessive alcohol consumption causes a person to lose control of their physical and mental faculties. When intoxicated, we can go insane and do things that aren't lawful. We may feel unable to move physically while under the influence of alcohol. Similarly, consuming extra spicy meals might induce a runny nose and tears in our eyes. With these two everyday situations, we can see how the food and drink that we consume affect both our minds and our bodies.

We should make sure that all macro- and micronutrients are available in our diet. Just eating food is not going to help us stay healthy. A good diet for us is a vegetarian diet. Archaeologists have recently found the bones of ancient gladiators (professional combatants in ancient Rome). The study reveals the fact, thanks to modern technology, that they were all vegans.

We, as humans, are meant to consume a vegetarian diet. Even though there are thousands of varieties of vegetables on our planet, we depend heavily on a few non-vegetarian foods like chicken, mutton, and beef. It has an impact not just on our health but also on the environment.

Our ancient scholars did substantial research on performance. They meticulously examined the body, mind, and soul. Yoga and Ayurveda both confirm that our bodies have three Gunas: sattvic, rajasic, and tamasic. When we are in a sattvic state, we will be more productive. The rest of the Gunas are bad for our minds and bodies. Each of these three Gunas is mainly influenced by our food.

A properly hydrated body is a healthy body. Our bodies depend on water to survive. Water makes up 70% of our bodies, and the proper balance of water and electrolytes in our bodies determines how well our internal systems function. Dehydration can slow down circulation and affect the flow of oxygen to our brains. When we are dehydrated, our bodies store more heat, which lowers our ability to tolerate hot temperatures. Even mild dehydration, a fluid loss of less than 2%, can impair memory, mood, focus, and reaction time.

Our bodies are made to move, not to sit still for long periods. We get bored when we sit for a long time but feel energized when we go for a short walk. Walking is a great way to supply more energy to our bodies. Walking improves our muscular endurance and straightens our bones. Walking lowers stress and strengthens the immune system. Additionally, it boosts our mental stamina. There are several other health benefits of walking. Sundar Pichai, the CEO of Google, said in an interview he used to walk considerably more than usual when striving to come up with new ideas.

Knowing how our bodies and biological systems work can help us live longer with more physical endurance.

A lot of energy is hidden in our emotions. **Emotional energy** is a measure of how confident we are in ourselves. Emotional energy determines how we feel about what's going on in our lives, work, and surroundings. Our entire lives depend on how we feel at any given time. This is why we are always recommended to control our emotions.

Dr David Hawkins conducted research on emotional energy and claimed we could quantify our emotional energy. His research shows that a person's log level in their magnetic field goes up when they feel emotionally better. According to his research, hatred, worry, shame, regret, despair, blame, and humiliation are the emotions that destroy us at the cellular level. More than anything else, how long we can hold back our reaction to anything will maintain emotional stability. (More details are in the title, "Emotional Intelligence").

Spiritual energy is often ignored. Throughout our lives, from childhood to old age, we learn and explore many things, but we often forget to explore the spiritual aspect of our lives. We cannot progress to a higher level of consciousness if we do not develop our spiritual energies. We are the sum of what we learn from school, work, and our surroundings. But being spiritual is about knowing ourselves through consciousness. It will help people become more honest, loyal, and trustworthy.

Spirituality helps us discover our life's purpose or meaning. During the Vedic times, our ancient scholars lived by the values of Satya, Dharma, and Ahimsa, which are manifestations of pure spiritual consciousness.

At the end of the day, we are not satisfied because none of our activities brings us peace. Peace comes from within when we can detach ourselves from the outside world for a period of time. When we tune our minds to a higher level of consciousness that transcends material reality, we shall find peace. Without spirituality, we cannot be at peace with ourselves and with the outside world.

Knowing how to keep these four energies in balance is essential for peak performance. All four energy sources are interconnected in many ways.

Moreover, we need a "high-performer mindset" like Cristiano Ronaldo. He has always aspired to be the best; thus, every day, he challenges himself a little more. Have you watched the Euro Cup 2020 pre-match interview where he removed two Coca-Cola bottles off the table and advised viewers to drink water instead? As a consequence of this gesture, the Coca-Cola Company suffered a four-billion-dollar loss.

It was neither a publicity stunt nor a planned act, but it was so genuine. His physical condition was put to the test when he moved from Real Madrid to Juventus. He was 35 years old at the time. Doctors estimated his fitness level was comparable to that of a 21-year-old boy. It is not a miracle. He has a strong conviction in maximizing performance.

Yoga, a sattvic diet, and enough rest will help to achieve good physical health; meditation, affirmations, and journaling help to build good mental strength. A positive mindset helps to regulate our emotional energy; helping and serving others will help us grow spiritually. If we wish to be star performers, we must carry out an assessment of our energy levels.

We all operate in either of three modes: boring, busy, or flow state. Have you ever felt you accomplished a lot in a short amount of time and were extremely happy? On other days, though, you may feel awful and be unable to do even a small amount of the task. We will become more productive when we work in flow, and we accomplish nothing when we work in a state of boredom or busyness.

We're bored at work because we're not interested in what we're doing. Each day we go to work without reason. Because they don't know how the job is done, almost all newly hired employees end up getting bored. Freshers who don't get enough training will always be confused. We make excuses when we're bored. We get bored at work when we feel alone and distant. Employees who collaborate and derive innovative solutions are much more committed to the process. The best way to change a boring environment is to look at how many ways you can do the same job.

Busyness is another way to describe our way of doing work. When we push employees to do more, they become busy. If there is no system to do the job or the system isn't improved, we need to work a lot to stay busy. Because of the lack of technological support, we perform a great amount of manual labour. When we don't divide the work equally, we are always busy at work.

Setting up a busy workplace is caused by managers who aren't good at their jobs, goals that aren't realistic, and not having enough planning for the work. To avoid busyness, we should not procrastinate or multitask. When we're busy, we tend to complain and point the finger at others. Being busy at work is a way to show off for many employees.

The distinction between being busy and being productive is significant. Being productive is the polar opposite of being busy all the time. We do not add value when we work in a state of boredom or busyness.

It is a tough goal to achieve in a flow state. We can easily shift people from boredom to busyness. Those who are high performers typically work in a state of flow. Flow refers to the amount of focus placed on a specific task. When in a flow state, we are fully absorbed in a task. The higher the level of clarity, the less effort it takes to enter a flow state.

A work environment that is full of distractions, multitasking, uncontested, and misery in the workplace will not lead to a flow state. According to ten-year research, people who work in a flow state are 500% more productive.

Researchers in both positive psychology and neuroscience have described what they call the "flow state." Our cognitive capacities are limited. The quality of the effort determines the quantity of concentration we devote to specific activities. To put it another way, if we wanted to work in a flow state, we had to eliminate distractions, be passionate about our job, and push ourselves beyond our comfort zones. If you work with less focus, the quality of your work will degrade.

Every year, Bill Gates takes two weeks off to reset his mind. He refers to this as "think week." He stays alone throughout this period, away from any distractions, somewhere in a forest. This is what it means to be in a flow state at work. He only carries a set of books, research, and scientific papers to spark new ideas. The think week was the source of many of his innovative ideas for his business, including the development of Internet Explorer in 1995.

A business is defined by the value it derives from its assets. The more time we spend in a flow state, the more value we create. How much value we can produce depends on how much control we have. And the overall value created by the work at a specific time is called "work done."

Everyone in your organization has a distinct set of skills. Everyone is qualified in their own unique way. However, hard work is scarce. I'd say it's not hard work but heart work, which is why it's hard to find. Nobody is willing to give their very best. No small business wants to treat its employees the best way possible. Fifty percent of performance issues are solved when the employees have the proper attitude towards their work and the company they work for. All performance issues are resolved when a company builds a suitable work culture. Inspiring leadership and value systems are more critical to improving performance.

Experience has a significant impact on personal performance. But in what sense do we use the term "experienced worker"? Let us explore.

Let's say it's been ten years since a young chef Ramu started making pizza. However, he believes one year of experience is enough for a chef like him. It is because he is relying on the repetition of the work rather than the quality of the work. Ramu stopped gaining experience as soon as he felt he knew enough.

After that, no matter how brilliant or competent he is, everything he does will be on autopilot mode. He won't be able to reach his full potential until he gets rid of this false perception. Even though Ramu has been making pizzas for ten years, he only has one year of experience and has spent the other nine years on autopilot. It is called the "experience illusion."

Our experience should get broader and deeper as we progress. Experience is something that always grows if we put deliberate effort into it; if we focus on both the quality and quantity of our experience. The best word to describe it is "upskilling."

We work hard to study theories but do not get the opportunity to apply them. We always believe that we know everything after learning a theory somewhere. It is comparable to learning how to swim online. You'll know how to move your arms and legs in the water, but it is impossible to prove in real life.

Practice everything you've learned to gain valuable experience; otherwise, all your knowledge will be useless. We can't achieve the quality of experience if we operate in autopilot mode. In autopilot mode, we have a repetitive quantity of experience but not a conscious quantity of experience.

The relevancy of your research, the quality of information you acquire, and your ability to use that knowledge to solve issues in real life are what determine the quality of your work, not how many times you do your job. Quality of experience has the power to change something reasonable, profitable, and beneficial. The quality of the experience depends on how many problems we can solve creatively and productively.

People who have the quality of experience never weigh everything equally. If you ask someone who doesn't have the quality of experience, they will tell you everything is important in life and business, because they failed to recognize the critical elements that contributed to long-term success.

The quality of your experience depends on which company you are working for. Without the best possible working conditions and challenges, employees will never be able to get a quality experience. The challenges you give your employees every day have a great impact on the quality of their experience.

In an elementary example, the quality of experience is like when you can send a rocket into outer space wherever you want, whereas the quantity of experience is when you can manufacture a rocket that is fit to travel.

Both play an important role in the workplace. But without adding a competitive element in both quantity and quality, no one can push their employees to the high-performance level.

A fixed mindset is a barrier to exploring new perspectives. People with fixed mindsets will not try anything new; they are scared of change. This mindset will negatively affect performance. They continually wait for the right moment until they realize every past moment was the right moment.

Ethics are important when it comes to performance. Ethics are a set of moral principles that must be followed for a community to function properly. Ethics are meant to support one another without causing harm to one another. In the same way, we must adhere to certain ideals in our professional lives, which are referred to as our work ethic. A strong work ethic will motivate employees to collaborate and work as a team to achieve a common goal. Management is responsible for setting up a strong work ethic. What message will a manager send to his staff if they arrive late every time at work?

Make yourself stand out. You can't duplicate other work ethics for your company. Take appropriate measures and experiment with new ideas that match your company's vision. Many companies strive to mimic the work ethics of other successful businesses, forgetting that people, processes, standards, values, culture, and vision differ from one organization to the next. It's easy to imitate but tough to implement.

Teamwork is influenced by our ethics and ideals. A brilliant performer with a lousy attitude will not add value to the team. It will not successfully operate if management is unable to communicate a suitable behaviour model. Many sportsmen and players have had their finest careers wrecked by bad conduct, such as steroid usage in the Olympics, match-fixing in cricket, or not performing effectively for their team.

The strength of oneness is unfathomable. An effective team is built on synergy. Synergy will aid in the exchange of ideas and experiences— everyone in the workplace benefits from synergy. A company's cohesiveness and growth are based on synergy. The degree of synergy in a company determines its overall performance.

Synergy helps you grow not only internally but also externally with your supply chain, consumers, and other organizations with whom you deal. Synergy brings discipline and consistency. For example, if you decide to go to the gym for the first time, you may quit after a month or so. However, if you plan to go to the gym with your partner or friends, you may have a better chance of staying a long time. This is the hidden power of synergy.

Soft skills help in the formation of strong connections and a sense of togetherness in the workplace. Soft skills help in the creation of hard skills. You can't influence people if you don't have strong soft skills. It will inevitably boost your capacity to take charge.

Soft skills are the foundation of company's reputation, such as problem-solving, creativity, communication skills, and so on. The more effort you put into improving your hard and soft skills, the happier you will be at work. The greater your happiness at work, the greater your productivity.

In performance, consistency is crucial. We should acknowledge our accomplishments in the past and place a high priority on improving them. Consistency requires deliberate practice in the right direction. You will be valued more than your competition only if your performance is consistent. Without consistency, it is impossible to improve anything in your company.

In a hypothetical situation, there is an auction taking place. For the auction, there are three participants. One of them is Cristiano Ronaldo, while the other two are players from well-known clubs. Who do you think will bag more money in the basket? Of course, Cristiano. This is the price for not only the performance but also the consistency. Your value and reputation will eventually decrease if you perform inconsistently.

The best performers always have job security and future growth, and they are respected by their peers. Opportunities await excellent performers, and they have the luxury to choose what they want, while others quit and search for jobs now and then.

When you have a lot on your plate, you'll be distracted and more likely to multitask, which is very counterproductive. It will negatively impact your performance. Delegate your job wisely to avoid multitasking.

Underperformers are always a result of bad leadership. When we have many underperformers, we should focus on the management policies and standards rather than the employees.

Ask each of your workers to answer three questions,

In the workplace, what do they fear most?

What do they appreciate most about the company?

What, if anything, do they think the company could do better?

If they can confidently respond to these questions, you can expect a better work culture.

If you do it with excellence, any job can be a way to change the world. Otherwise, everything will be the same.

"The god of fortune is karma"

The Art of Connection: Communication

---•---

Words possess magical powers. Words have the power to make you or break you. You will lose your credibility in a split second if you speak wrongly. If you speak wisely, your words can develop trust and confidence in a second. No matter who you are or what you do, the way you communicate reveals your professional capacity and personality. You can always come out on top if you know what to say and how to say it in any given situation.

Why is it said that communication is an art? Communication is an expression, and any form of expression is an art. Your ability to express yourself is crucial for effective communication. In other words, communication is your only opportunity to showcase your abilities to the outside world.

When we talk to someone, they will try to absorb and interpret the information in their own way. Oftentimes, the intent behind our message might be misconstrued. If our message confuses the listener, it either means our method of communication is ineffective or the listener understood it as the opposite. In both cases, the person who wants to convey the message suffers a loss. To reduce the effect of miscommunication, we should add more clarity to our message, like by telling a story.

For instance, how do you teach math to a child? You will display images, videos, and real objects. But would you consider the same method while teaching math to high school students? Of course not. This comprehension is the foundation of any effective communication. Know your audience well, know your message inside out, and finally, simplify what you want to say.

The communication is deemed successful when the audience truly grasps the information without repeated explanations. If you have trouble convincing people what you want, that's a big mistake. This is known as miscommunication. Eighty percent of the time, we miscommunicate with each other. Our relationships with others will be weakened and rendered meaningless by miscommunication.

Communication is the combination of words (verbal) and actions (non-verbal). Nonverbal communication is as important as verbal communication, perhaps more important. Rather than trying to avoid difficult situations, a genuine smile can sometimes calm us down. Poor nonverbal communication will negatively affect our personalities. When we talk to someone, for example, they feel so uncomfortable if we don't look into their eyes. According to studies, nonverbal communication builds up 55% of the impression we make. Facial expressions, body postures, and eye contact are considered nonverbal communication.

What is more striking, the lengthy gratitude speech of an Oscar award winner or Mr Bean snatching the Oscar and walking off the stage without speaking a single word? Which of these two situations do you remember even after a long time? We all still remember Mr Bean leaving the stage without saying a word. This exemplifies the power that lies behind nonverbal communication.

Many aspects of our daily lives rely on our ability to communicate non-verbally. The research was conducted on married couples to find out what drives them to stay together for many years. A happy marriage is the result of strong nonverbal communication. For example, don't try to help your partner solve their problems based on how you think they should be solved. Instead, you should offer them emotional support to get through their difficulties.

One important aspect of good communication is being able to listen. Why is it important for everyone to develop listening skills? Not only to hear what people are saying but also to absorb what they are attempting to communicate. In every conversation, there are two parts: what is said and what isn't. When you listen to others actively, you can figure out what is being said and what isn't. In Korean schools, students aren't allowed to ask questions in the middle. Students can only ask a question when the whole session is over. If you ask questions in the middle of a lecture, the whole class will be distracted. What if your questions get answered in the following chapters?

Here's why I think it is crucial to listen actively: When I was interviewing a candidate for a company, I asked about his previous income. He began telling me a story about something other than his income. He said, "Sir, I get a very less salary there, and so does everyone else. I had a hard time getting a pay raise. I am unable to satisfy my financial obligations. Everyone is leaving there because the company doesn't pay as much as other companies. "

He did not specify his compensation in figures, but he wanted me to guess he is seeking a higher wage. In the scenario mentioned above, I cared the least about how much that company paid its employees. This is what is called over-speaking. When we don't listen attentively, we end up talking too much for no reason.

People will like and respect you more if you are willing to listen to them intently. When you speak, you only communicate what you know. It won't help you much to understand the world outside. But if you listen, you will learn many new things, some of which could be turning points in your life.

Communication is a crucial skill to master, regardless of your profession. The better your communication skills, the greater your chances of advancing in your professional journey. In a Stanford survey, over 10,000 highly successful Stanford alums were asked about their successful careers. All of them agreed that soft skills—in particular, the ability to communicate effectively—were the catalyst behind their phenomenal success.

In a business context, communication is all about interacting with each other with the help of systems, policies, standards, emails, interviews, messages, meetings, circulars, and so on. All of these methods of communication are formal. It defines authority in order to enhance work cooperation. It shows how information flows from top to bottom and bottom to top, from one worker to another, and from one department to another.

But we should also look for ways to communicate with each other informally. To make the relationship healthy and valuable, we need to spend time together in a casual way, such as by doing fun activities, holding informal meetings, and arranging leisure trips.

As per my research, there are four reasons why we should improve communication skills in the workplace.

To create a win-win situation; to create a happy and positive place to work:

When you and your kid are walking down the street, your kid asks for a toy. You don't want to waste your money on toys that can be broken in a day, and you try to convince your kid that it's not a good toy. But your kid cries stubbornly. To stop crying, you get your kid some yummy chocolate.

Finally, both are satisfied and have returned home. Who is the winner here? You didn't want to spend money on toys that were likely to break within a day. The kid was happy because he got his favourite chocolate. This is how we should find a solution that benefits everyone. It is called a win-win situation. It is something that everyone is looking forward to.

You can't yell at your workers all the time and expect them to do what you want. Only a few people would stay with you if they knew they couldn't find work anywhere else. The good ones will leave you and go somewhere else, where they will be listened to and appreciated. This is the only way to build synergy so everyone can benefit in the long run.

Do remember that you can't achieve your goals on your own. Your organization's goal can only be met with the help of good, talented employees. The key to growth is ensuring that everyone around you is smarter and more intelligent than you. You have a good education and skill set, but what if you fail to develop a win-win situation because of your poor communication skills? You will struggle all your life because of this.

There are some managers who barely communicate with their employees. If you don't connect with them, how can they connect with you? How you can work together even if you don't know or understand each other.

Understanding and respecting one another, valuing one another's views and suggestions, giving your employees freedom, communicating without boundaries, and providing proper training and appropriate feedback all contribute to the development of win-win situations.

To avoid filtration; to be in a positive feedback loop, and to get better every day:

Let's assume you have ten employees working for you, and you are the company owner. Whenever you want any information, you depend particularly on one person. You only trust one person to find out what's going on in your company. Then 90% of the information you receive will be filtered.

Everyone in the company is focused on short-term benefits. This means the person who is sharing the information will filter all the information according to what he or she wants to say, not what everyone else wants to say. You do not get a clear picture of the matter when it reaches you. The answer will have a 1:10 ratio of the correct information.

Without correct information, you will make decisions that benefit only a few people and not the company as a whole. This will result in a great deal of confusion and misunderstanding within the organization. The best way to avoid filtration is to develop a very inclusive communication channel. No one in the company will be left behind without listening to them.

If you don't avoid filtration, unity will not be maintained. There is no harmony in the workplace when there is no unity. Once harmony is broken, there is no possibility of trust. Trust is what makes things happen. Trust must be maintained at all costs if you want to achieve any results.

You will never receive honest feedback if you do not avoid filtering. Being in the correct feedback loop is a blessing for both personal and professional life. An organization is the collective force of systems, standards, people, machines, and so on. Without a doubt, if you are unable to receive accurate feedback, you are spiralling downward. When you receive the right feedback, you can either fix the problem right away and start a better day tomorrow or will continue doing your job the same way.

Feedback can only be given in data form. Do not submit your feedback in any other informal way. It should be like showing statistics after a football match. How much does a team possess in the ball, shots, passes, shots on target, and accuracy? This type of feedback will help build an efficient improvement strategy.

An error-free and stress-free culture; to reduce mistakes and accidents:

The more efficiently you communicate with your employees, the more you can expect an error-free culture. I would like to tell you that being error-free and stress-free is a culture, not a standard. Suppose you have an international system and keep the highest standards at your workplace. If you don't connect well with everyone, you won't be able to yield the benefits.

We cannot solve problems when there is a communication gap. In a lot of instances, we receive the same problems repeatedly. It is certain that if any problem recurs, there must be a communication gap. Try to understand the problem with an effective communication method. First, find the problem, ask what the problem is, and know if the problem really exists. Gather more evidence to prove that the problem is real and needs to be fixed. How do you do it? Conduct a brainstorming session. Initiate a small group activity.

Employees feel stressed at work if the working culture is not supportive. Upliftment should be an integral part of the working culture. Having compassion for others is essential for teaming up, which benefits everyone involved. If management gave employees the necessary freedom to make decisions, their potential would automatically improve. Over the past few decades, this concept has benefited a wide range of large businesses. Most small businesses, however, are hesitant to implement this.

Clarity and transparency are the outcomes of an error-free workplace. The reluctance to change stems from a lack of clarity. In small businesses, mid and bottom-level employees are working with a lot of confusion, which leads to unnecessary delays, quality issues, and delivery issues that are considered "normal".

Employees are not invited to participate in the decision-making process. In most companies, general managers independently make decisions on quality or production without even informing the department in charge or supervisors.

A fine example of a confused workspace is when we see the number **18** from our side, and the person on the opposite side sees it as **81**. A manager always assumes he is good and correct, so he will never attempt to see the number 81. We should always consider other people's views to run a happy business.

We should let our workers know what work is important and what needs to be done right away. The distinction between important and urgent work should be very clear to everyone. Workplace transparency is directly proportional to the level of communication between employees and management.

There are over thirty lean tools that all communicate well to eliminate errors in the workplace. For instance, the lean tool poka-yoke has been developed to avoid human error while working. It will help us spot possible mistakes in a workflow. A car has many safety features, which are all examples of poka-yoke. When your car door is open, you will hear a beep sound that acts as a reminder to close it properly. Exactly like this, an error-free standard will function.

Influence and persuasion; to get what you want:

If you want to listen and follow, you need some qualities in default mode. If Cristiano Ronaldo advised us to get vaccinated against the coronavirus, many of us would do. But no one cares if the WHO director tells us to do so. Your influence will be determined by your personality, looks, behaviour, communication skills, capability in certain positions, and achievements.

If you are tough with your employees, they will think they are being abused. They do not feel an authentic connection with you. You must be highly critical of your processes, but not on your workers. Instead of criticizing the workers, help them improve the systems by providing them with the resources to do so. It works well only if you can influence your workers.

When managing a business, we must cultivate positive relationships with employees, clients, vendors, and suppliers. Every business arrangement we make must contribute to our prosperity. Negotiate each contract so as to earn a profit. To make a structural change, you'll need to strike a deal with your workforce.

You can influence anyone if you can connect with them at their level. You should be a skilled storyteller if you want to persuade your employees. Make them feel like they're an important part of your company. When they're with the management, make them feel comfortable.

We should practice patience when dealing with our employees. First, gain your employees' trust, and then they will work for you. Script a good reason why your employees should work for you. Create a strong emotional bond with your employees.

For example, politicians try their best to pursue our votes. Moreover, half of our Lok Sabha members have criminal records. The majority of our politicians are corrupt. The majority of our elected political leaders are uneducated. The vast majority of our politicians come from political families and run their political parties like family businesses. Nonetheless, we vote for them. We support them blindly. We pay attention to them. We listened to them. Why? They know how to tell a good story to get you to feel what they want you to feel.

Communication skills are the key to connecting and influencing others. Spend quality time with co-workers once a week or once a month, so you can find out what is going on in their lives at work. Make time to get to know your employees and their problems. Sit with a high performer for an hour or more every week. Make them feel proud.

Those who care the most will get what they want. Things will begin to favour those with more interesting stories to tell. The market will shift toward those with greater advantages. Whoever can make the best content will always come out on top.

Here are some studies that show how important it is to have good communication skills,

Employees who believe that managers listen to them are twenty times more likely to feel loyal to the company.

More than 80% of the problems in the company are due to miscommunication.

More than 40% of employees believe there is no transparency in the company.

More than 96% of employees want a more empathetic approach to communication.

Nearly 70% of workplaces would be more productive with effective communication in the workplace.

Companies with effective communication programs are four times more likely to outperform the competition.

More than 40% of employees think there is not enough collaboration.

The proper way to talk to someone is to listen 80% of the time and talk 20% of the time. This is a skill that can be learned and mastered through training and practice.

Good communication will significantly reduce the need for daily meetings.

Below are some suggestions for improving your communication skills in the workplace, Be more receptive.

Prepare everything before a formal meeting. Be polite; use data, provide proof and facts, and share your observations.

Do not interrupt the talk. Don't speak as if you know everything. You get the best results when you listen more and think before you speak.

Communication is not sitting together in a meeting room and trying to prove I am the best. It is easy to find faults and mistakes in others. Communication is not for blaming each other. Rather, it is for coming up with best solutions and producing innovative ideas.

Good communication helps people share ideas, express how they feel, give feedback, and create a positive work environment. You should schedule a day once or twice a month when employees can get together and talk about whatever interests them.

There are many magical words; keep using these words to make a ripple effect. You look great today; you are a hard worker here; the company is indebted to your talent; yes, you are correct; many thanks for your dedication; I see our company's future in your hands; and so on.

One day, I was in a company. The manager was really angry over an employee who had made a mistake. He asked the manager what he should do to solve the problem, but the manager repeatedly denied his request. "I don't know; you must do it perfectly. This is why I hired you," said the manager. What if, instead, the manager understood and helped him figure out how to do the job right?

If you can't connect with people well enough, you will never get what you want. Without this timeless skill, you'll never achieve success, no matter how hard you work, how well you're educated, or how much experience you have.

You have a great product and service, but what if you fail to make a strong connection? You will not survive for a long time.

The first rule of effective communication is self-connection. We are disconnected from ourselves. We have no idea what we want; therefore, we make no effort to express it. Make sure you have a good connection with yourself before you try to connect with the outside world.

If you are an effective communicator, people will trust you, follow you, and pay attention to you. People will sincerely seek your help. Your opinion will be given more weight than anyone else's. You'll feel better about yourself. You feel more at ease working in any environment. You can learn things more quickly. You can develop solid ties with anyone. You will work without boundaries.

Recruitment And Beyond

"Show me your employees, and I can tell how your business will do in the future." It is not the computer that makes our work faster and easier; it is the people who worked so hard to make this machine work for us. We can talk to anyone and watch funny videos on our mobile phones because great minds once dreamed of that idea. It is not the rocket that takes us to and from the moon; it is the people that make this all work.

A few decades ago, hiring was not a priority in a business. At that time, all the jobs were straightforward. Customers had no choice, as we have today. Employers make hiring judgments based on a candidate's prior work experience and academic qualifications. This is still the norm for all small businesses.

Today, the business operates in a very different environment. Customers want services to be delivered quickly, comfortably, and affordably. Creative solutions are needed rather than a logical approach. Skill is more valuable than a fancy degree. The most sought-after characteristics of an ideal worker are the capacity to think creatively, solve multi-level problems, and communicate effectively.

Assume you have trouble attracting talent. Then undoubtedly, your recruiting strategy is flawed. If you haven't figured out how to hire someone who can contribute to your company's success, you don't know what you want from your employees. You are just presuming that you need employees to run your daily operations. With this mindset, you will always hire the wrong person, resulting in a significant loss. The purpose of recruitment is to identify qualified candidates who are a good fit for your company today and tomorrow.

As per the research, a bad hire will cost you the annual salary of the employee. This revealed the fact that if you offer a candidate 25,000 rupees per month and the candidate turns out to be a bad hire, you will lose 300,000 rupees. To avoid such big losses, keep in mind that you have complete control before hiring. The choice is yours!

To take decisions on hiring, you must first understand your company's future needs, the present skill and experience gap, market dynamics, and finally, the conditions of the recruiting process. This is something no one wants to do. Trying to save money on hiring is the worst thing you can do for your company. It is like you are on a journey to space and are not concerned about the rocket you are supposed to travel in.

If you want to save money on hiring, you're constantly on the lookout for people who will work for minimal remuneration. Low-cost hiring always results in low-cost outcomes, and this is basic logic. The best employees have already been hired and are working for the best organizations. The low-cost employees will create more problems than coming up with solutions.

It is our choice whether to work with below-average, mediocre, or talented individuals. Working with an average one is easy because they are mostly available. Make sure your hiring approach is well-placed if you want to work with skilled employees.

When you work with average people, you will always operate slowly. What if someone is smart enough to hire good employees all the time? What do you think? Do you think you'll ever be able to compete with them?

Most of us think delivery is the point of customer satisfaction and growth strategy. So, we employ mediocre talent to get the job done, not to improve the business. This notion must be abandoned.

Do not hire someone to do a small portion of the work; rather, hire someone who can solve multiple problems and set high standards. If Google hires people who can work only for their search engine, they can't reach the level they are at today. Multi-skilled and multi-talented professionals are required today for sustainable, speedy growth.

For example, if you own a restaurant, keeping waiters just to serve the orders is not a good idea. Hire someone who can smile at customers, maintain good hygiene, ask about food quality and feedback, make customers comfortable, and make them feel like they've been treated like kings and queens. This increases the likelihood that customers will return to your doorsteps.

Today, a person with a good idea helps companies better than someone with good experience.

What we need from our employees is complete ownership of whatever they do. To get the most out of any employee, ensure their total participation in the process. Forward-thinking employees are real assets, and they deserve to be treated well. Measure your employees in terms of the value they create for your company and for the customer, not how much you pay them.

People who want a job are easy to find, but people who love their jobs are harder to find. "Looking for job candidates" are unsatisfied workers who will seek employment elsewhere if they do not find comfort in their current position. They often boast about their abilities, which they don't have. All they care about is getting paid on time. Candidates who "love their work" are very interested in their work. Salary is only one aspect of their career. They have bigger aspirations for their careers. They stay where they can learn and grow.

Those who love their job will always produce positive results because they work while enjoying it. They are willing to do challenging work even if the resources are limited. Even if all resources are accessible, employees won't be satisfied if they don't enjoy the work.

When you hire someone, you make two bets. At first, you expect the individual will remain with your organization and contribute to your future success. The second bet is you believe they will make greater use of the resources available. In the first scenario, you put all your faith in the candidate. What would you do if the employee fell short of your expectations? The company's efficiency will drop, and you will be frustrated. In the second scenario, if the newcomer mismanages the resources, your return on investment (ROI) will diminish. The synergy will disintegrate if a new employee does not collaborate with the existing team members. The company's growth will suffer because of this.

Every time we hire someone, we always complain we can't find anyone who is the right fit for the job. Do you know the reason why it is difficult to get a good fit most of the time? Two types of data are filtered during the interview process that nobody cares about.

When we interview the candidate, they will tell their story with several filters that help them get the job. Research says more than 96% of candidates are ready to tell lies to get selected. (First-level filtration).

When you ask their previous employer, they will give you a different story with a few more filtrations according to their interests and experience with the candidate. (Second-level filtration).

The real story, without any filtration, is beyond these two stories. Only time and circumstance will uncover the original story.

We must also know the disparity in knowledge, skill, attitude, and experience will affect teamwork and performance. For example, there are five people working in one of your departments. One has 15 years of experience, two are freshers, one has two years of experience, and one has experience in a different field.

The gap between their experiences and knowledge will affect company productivity.

The guy with the most experience will have trouble dealing with the co-workers who have less experience. They will have different ideas about how they should function. The person with more experience will think that their way of doing things is the right way, while the person with less experience will think that the person with more experience is old-fashioned.

Have you ever thought about why it's so easy for you to hire someone? There are two reasons behind it. The first is that you are thinking of replacing the position. If you cannot understand the strengths of the employee, you cannot successfully replace them. We cannot extract work from the new hire. Always remember that you are replacing a person, not a position. Replace the person in the job with someone more skilled and talented to avoid making bad hires.

An engineer was very good at production planning activities in a company. He quit working there after a few years. He was replaced by another production engineer. But the new hire lacks skills in planning activities. Productivity went down drastically. Not because the ex-employee was the only person who could do the job but because the replacement was done in the wrong way. The company had to fire that new hire later. This cycle will continue until we capture every employee's skill and ability at work.

The second reason is that we are the most labour-intensive nation; thus, we don't take our hiring process seriously. We will never be short on employees; we know it. During interviews, many managers showed me hundreds of resumes on the waiting list. They all proudly told me, "Even if the most productive employee leaves the company, I can call a hundred candidates within an hour." But in hindsight, we would say, "Oh! That was a bad choice."

One thing you can do to refine your interview process is to record a video of the entire interview. This has a lot of benefits. You can watch it many times to decide if it's a good option. You can send this recording to an expert to get their advice on hiring decisions. It's in your record, and you can show them what a candidate accepted during the interview and for what they got the job. You can confirm whether the resume and real personality are a match or not. Get at least three person's opinions before making the final decision.

Also, asking for a "failure resume" (a resume with details of failures) along with a regular resume is a good idea. If a person is aware of their failures and mistakes, they will perform their best at any job.

It is not enough to take interviews during hiring time but take frequent interviews. To test consistency at work, take interviews three months later, six months later, and so on. If a person is making progress, then they are practicing well. They are reliable. Do this exercise not to fire your employees but to know the gap. The frequent interviews will reflect what a candidate needs to improve and what they are doing at work every day.

Write on your notice board, "When you pass your 50th interview, you will become indispensable." You can also use a noticeboard to communicate your company's requirements and the qualities you anticipate in your employees.

Apart from the usual interview questions, add the following questions.

What was your biggest contribution to the last company you worked for?

What are the main five challenges you faced, and how did you overcome them?

How do you solve problems?

Your setbacks and valuable lessons you gained from them?

How can your knowledge, experience, and skill sets contribute to the growth of my company?

How can my company help you in achieving your career goals?

Can we categorize our employees according to their working styles? Sure, we can. Employees are collaborating with us in two ways. There is, in fact, a third type. However, I do not want to discuss the third type. The two types are **"Responsible workers"** and **"Skilled workers"**. The third type is merely there for entertainment; they are not even considered employees. They show up in the morning, wander around, gossip, and then leave on time. They are aware that management will fire them at any time, but they are unconcerned.

They disregard company rules and values and defy authority. Attitude is their worst enemy. So, we will only discuss the two main types that I mentioned above.

Responsible worker style	**Skilled worker style**
Confused	Good communicator
Disciplined	Ethics
Task-oriented	Goal oriented
Blame	Never complain
Count days	Measure progress
Experience matters	Career matters
Hard skill focused	Soft skill focused
Unaware	Lifelong learner
Afraid to take challenges	Always take challenges
Unsatisfied	Happy
Unreliable	Reliable
Replaceable	Irreplaceable
Liability in long term	Always an asset
Work from the side, middle, and end	Prioritize
Follow instructions	Explore options
Follow the routine	Meticulous
Not committed	Highly committed

Reactive	Proactive
Responsible	Ownership
Fixed mindset	Growth mindset
Not add any value	Add value to employer, customer, and self
Comfort zone	Pushing limits
Outdated	Specialist
Resistance to change	Always evolve
Repeat the mistakes	Reduces the mistakes
Focus on problems	Come up with solutions

Now you may have realized how a skilled worker and a responsible worker differ from one another. A responsible worker works with responsibility, and a skilled worker work with ownership. It's okay to be a responsible employee. But it's not a good idea to continue being a responsible worker.

A responsible worker can easily transition to a skilled worker if they focus and work hard enough. Moving from being responsible to being a skilled worker is a shared responsibility. What colleges don't teach, what we can't learn ourselves, in companies, we can.

Sometimes it can be tricky to know who is a responsible and skilled worker. From the above data, a responsible worker may be a good communicator too. Being a good communicator does not imply that they are a skilled worker. However, it shows that they can very quickly transition into skilled workers.

A skilled worker adds value to the employer, the customer, and themselves. When the business benefits from the skilled employee, the employer will return the favour. As a result, skilled workers benefit greatly everywhere. It is a continuous cycle of value.

When I asked employees about their performance during my research, many of them defended themselves and told me, "I'm the best employee here, but the company doesn't give me any chances to shine." My only response is that you are lying for no reason; talent cannot be hidden. Skill is visible. Prove yourself first. If the talent cannot be recognized, we will never see anyone come up as a champion.

During my research, many managers told me that many good workers had left there for no good reason. Why do some good workers quit their job very soon? It is not because your company isn't good; it is about the working culture of your organization.

Good employees want to do their best with an open mind, but the politics and ad culture won't let them do it. The politics and culture of the company make it difficult for them to function effectively for any newcomer or a skilled employee. It is a well-established fact that a good worker cannot survive in a negative environment.

Conduct a meeting on recruitment every year. List out what went wrong and who is a fast learner; who is a bottleneck; what market trends exist; what skills need to be added for long-term success; and what type of person is required. Then fire someone who is not adding value and look for someone who could probably be the best fit for you.

Describe ten desirable attributes in a candidate based on your interests and market demands. A candidate who receives 7 out of 10 will be an excellent pick.

Finally, ask the most interesting question. Do we really need this number of employees? Who is going to fill those gaps if we lay off some low performers? If our government amended the labour law and doubled the wages, would you continue to work with the same employees?

A person who is smarter than others will find a way to complete the job as fast as possible.

A person who is more intelligent than others can solve problems better than others.

A person who has a good attitude will have a good work ethic.

A person who has a good experience will have the necessary knowledge of how to do the work.

A person who has a growth mindset will always improve their skills and knowledge base.

Emotional Intelligence: A Superpower

What emotions are you experiencing now as you read this book? Don't overthink it; just scribble it down. If you can't, you'll have to figure it out. Whatever we do, we must be aware of our emotions; otherwise, we are no different from other animals. Without emotional intelligence, our chances of achieving success in life are nil.

A recent study estimates automation and artificial intelligence will eliminate 300 to 400 million jobs in the future. Empathy, emotional intelligence, creativity, and problem-solving skills will not be automated or replaced in the future. Artificial intelligence and automation can eliminate all repetitive tasks, but it seems unlikely that a computer will ever learn to be imaginative or empathetic.

In a recent interview, Facebook founder Mark Zuckerberg acknowledged that it is difficult to find employees with both EQ and IQ. However, he emphasized that the EQ, not the IQ, is critical to a person's long-term success in the workplace.

Before we look at emotional intelligence, we should know what intelligence is. We often misperceive the concept of intelligence. If someone does well on an exam, we think he or she is very intelligent. We believe intelligent people are those who qualify for IAS or JEE exams or get jobs in big companies like Google or Tesla. This is a wrong idea that we have about intelligence. An intelligent person has nothing to do with passing exams or getting a job. Anyone can make it. Anyone who is prepared enough can become an IAS officer or a doctor. This is called "competitiveness," not intelligence.

Competitiveness is necessary for survival; it has nothing to do with intelligence. Being highly competitive means you are a hero in the eyes of a few but not in the eyes of the world. Becoming intelligent, however, is a whole different ball game. To put it simply: only intelligent people can change the world. It is beyond our capabilities and expertise. Intelligent people will never chase temporary happiness or greatness; instead, they work for the greater goal of making the world a better place to live.

We are all born free, but there are chains everywhere. Those who have the courage to break the chains will only develop intelligence. A person who is shackled by money, relationships, religion, position, or even their thoughts can never become intelligent.

Mahatma Gandhi was a very intelligent man. How can a person devote his whole life to defending the truth? An ordinary person cannot conceive that the mighty British army can be defeated using nonviolent efforts. But Mahatma Gandhi proved it.

Nikola Tesla was an intelligent man. He changed the way people in those days thought about energy and electricity. How could he believe that AC would change the course of history without testing it on an industrial scale?

Isaac Newton was born into a family where no one had any science background. He was a below-average student at school. Yet he transformed the world of science. Very few people throughout history possessed any intelligence. The others are all peer-trained people. Learning how to read, write, and how to work hard is all about training. Trained people and intelligent people are very different. An intelligent person devotes their life to a purpose that could change the world.

Try this experiment to see the difference between intelligence and competitiveness. Give a book to 10 participants, then conduct a test ten days later. Everything in a single volume is easy to learn and remember. Next time, give them two volumes and conduct an exam ten days later, which is also not so hard. But what if we give one hundred books to those ten participants and conduct a test ten days later?

In this case, someone will score higher marks depending on how much time they spend on it, their hard-working method, who is helping them to learn, what they remember during the exam, the quality of resources they have, how good they are at writing the content, and the most important thing is the focus. It has nothing to do with intelligence. It's all about being competitive and willing to put in hard work.

You can't change anything if you pass difficult exams, earn a good degree, or are born into a well-to-do family. It matters how much you can inspire and help others; what you can do to change the world for the better is a measure of real intelligence. With your effort, if you can change the course of history, you will be considered intelligent. Intelligence is when you leave behind your signature. If your actions can predict the future, you are an intelligent person without a doubt.

(You can be an activist, but never on the same level as Mahatma Gandhi. you can be an inventor but never like Nikola tesla. You can be a spiritual master, but you can never be as great as Swamy Vivekananda if you lack real intelligence).

During my research, a manager once told me he was a very good worker in his early years. After many years of hard work, he is now a manager of the company. He then told me he didn't know how to get along with his employees and customers. When things went wrong, he always became agitated.

He often fired his employees for no good reason. Every day, he strived to be an effective leader for the entire organization. He wasn't sure what he should do to get the best results. He's missing something that was very detrimental. All he was referring to was his lack of emotional intelligence. It is not just his story; more than 90% of managers shared the same experience with me.

Emotional Intelligence: A Superpower

Daniel Goleman's best-selling book, Emotional Intelligence, completely changes the way how we think about life and leadership. He did a study to find out why some people are highly successful in business and life while others are not, despite having very good knowledge and experience, After many years of research, he finally confirmed that EQ, not IQ is the decisive factor for a successful life. Emotional intelligence is the ability to recognize, control, and deal with our feelings in all situations, as well as to understand and acknowledge the feelings and values of others.

It is one of the hardest skills to learn but also the most rewarding. According to a study, our intelligence quotient (IQ) accounts for approximately 20% of our accomplishments, whereas emotional intelligence accounts for 80%. EI will help us give and receive feedback, deal with change in an organization, and meet deadlines. EI will empower us to deal with problems and setbacks. It will also help us deal with people who are hard to get along with.

There are several tests we can take today to find out how emotionally intelligent we are. Self-report and ability tests are the two main types. The focus of a self-report is on our strengths and weaknesses. An ability test is for recognizing and controlling our own and other people's feelings.

Why is emotional intelligence so important in the workplace today? It is difficult to get along in life and at work if we don't recognize and regulate how we feel and act. Emotions might induce us to act rashly, resulting in a snowball effect in the workplace.

EI will help us talk to each other in a way that doesn't hurt anyone. EI will enable us to deal with our feelings when we're stressed. It will help us get along with our co-workers and customers and solve a problem without creating another one. If you can solve every conflict, your employees will look up to you as role models and great leaders.

It is impossible to manage our emotions entirely. However, losing control of our emotions is just too risky. We are always talking with other humans, not with machines. We can't speak to people as if they don't have any feelings. Knowing when to hold off reacting is crucial in building a long-term relationship. In reality, not every situation requires a response.

Everyone has their share of frustrations in life. People working in small businesses have a hard time making ends meet. It would make a big difference in their lives if you, as a manager, took an empathetic attitude toward their problems. If people think you are kind and generous, they will do everything they can when times are hard.

People will not change for us, even if we want them to. We're unhappy at work because we can't keep our employees under our control. We anticipate a certain level of performance, but in fact, it is different from reality. Reality is what you are now confronted with. If the quality of your products and services are poor, this is the reality. Accept it immediately. Customers will leave you if you do not accept reality. You cannot anticipate change until you first become the change you want.

You are responsible for what others say about you and to you. As a manager, you should keep your authority and sense of self-respect. Make others express themselves so that you can listen to them more clearly.

Four elements make EI complete: self-awareness knows what we are thinking; social awareness is total awareness of where we are; self-management is how to control our emotions, and relationship management is how we deal with others.

Self-awareness:

It is the capacity to comprehend our emotions with great clarity. In the course of developing self-awareness, we will learn how to observe our emotions. The process of self-awareness involves knowing our pleasant and unpleasant emotions and how to handle them in a better way.

When you are aware of what you think and feel in every situation, it is easy to identify your strengths and weaknesses. It is the most crucial ability for a manager to have. If you don't know what your strengths and weaknesses are, how will you lead a team and your company? To know your weaknesses and strengths, be aware of what triggers you to make decisions in any given situation.

Everyone has innate skills and abilities. Otherwise, Bill Gates' daughter might have been the most talented person on the planet. He can arrange all the resources available today at his disposal to make his daughter the most skilled and perfect person in the world. We can learn any skill, but we cannot outperform it unless we are naturally built for it. Therefore, it is critical to understand our strengths and weaknesses.

Our lack of self-awareness is to blame for the average quality of our lives; we have no idea what our best qualities are and how we may improve.

If you are not aware of your emotions, you will end up causing lots of conflicts within and around you. As a result, you grow increasingly stressed. You make every decision and choice based on how you feel rather than what the actual requirements are. As a result, you make poor judgments most of the time. Therefore, you will become the most disliked manager.

Over time, self-awareness helps us become more self-confident. Some people think they can do everything because of overconfidence. You become increasingly arrogant and egotistical over time if you assume you can handle everything on your own. You don't need to be overly or underconfident if you rely on your skills and abilities. Confident individuals have a greater proclivity toward learning, problem-solving, and helping others.

To become self-confident, you need to know the gap between being overconfident and being underconfident. Fear of the unknown, lack of preparedness, criticism, and lack of knowledge are the main reasons for low confidence.

Ask yourself why you are jealous of anything the next time you feel it. The next time when you find yourself laughing, ask yourself why. Ask yourself why you are feeling so depressed. Your journey toward developing emotional intelligence will advance if you can identify the causes of your feelings. Self-awareness is understanding why you feel the way you feel. Once you understand the cause, you can control the effect.

Self-management:

Biological impulses drive our emotions. We cannot live away from them, but we can regulate them. Self-regulation is important in leaders because people who can reasonably control their emotions can foster an environment of trust and fairness. Our emotions are out of sync with the situation most of the time. Developing emotional intelligence will help us overcome those situations.

Self-regulation is so essential for competitive reasons. Business today is rife with ambiguity and change. Technology transforms work at a dazzling pace. Only people who have mastered their emotions can easily adapt to a change and get along with any situation.

It doesn't imply that we ought to learn to repress our emotions. It is to be aware of the ideal circumstances for expressing our emotions. Being a human involves, having emotions are a natural process. Don't deny it; accept it. Sigmund Freud once quoted, "Unexpressed emotions never die; they are buried alive and will come forth later in uglier ways."

Anger is the most destructive emotion we all have. Those who are angry are always in danger. Let's imagine that someone has provoked you. How do you react to this situation? Do you react right away, or do you pause for some time to recognize it? Try to understand the situation rather than judge it. Every feeling eventually fades away. It can be managed and understood in a matter of seconds. You will always be more composed and rational if you can control your emotions, and for a manager, it is a crucial skill to learn.

If we know how to channel our anger, it can do amazing things. Here is an example from my own life. My wife was so lazy and reluctant to learn to drive. Once, we had a terrible accident, which stopped her from learning to drive. Every time I pushed her to learn to drive, her emotional brain connected to the accident, and she was really frightened of driving. However, she began to learn. One day I was teaching her when she made a mistake at a traffic signal. I struck her head. At that time, she was very angry.

That day she vowed to learn to drive in a week to prove that she could drive the car without my help. And she succeeded. She did not learn to drive for three years, but in seven days, she did it. That is the power of anger when it can channel properly.

I recall talking to my friend, who had a terrible temper. I once advised him if he couldn't control his anger, he would suffer greatly later in life. But his response was hilarious. He told me, "Man, James Cameroon is a very angry person. Steve Jobs was also a very angry person, so why shouldn't I be?" I was surprised, not because of his reply, but because people often justify their faults by comparing them to those of great people.

James Cameron and Steve Jobs had good reason to be angry. At the beginning of their careers, they were never angry. They have worked so hard their whole lives to make something so innovative, valuable, and inspiring. To build the legacy they left behind, they had to dedicate their entire lives and endure countless sacrifices. For them, getting angry when anything goes wrong is normal.

Not only does anger need to be regulated, but every emotion does, too. We have often witnessed fans fighting after a soccer game due to their disappointment in their team's performance. Once you know the reason behind your emotions, you can control and channel them effectively. When we observe our emotions, they will move from our reptilian brain to the neocortex, which will help us to make conscious decisions. It is the science behind self-regulation.

If you are not able to control your emotions yourself, you will always find yourself in situations where others control your life.

Social awareness:
Have you ever felt like you didn't belong somewhere? Because of our poor social skills, we often feel out of place. Without being the right fit, we can't expect anyone to do anything for us.

When you are completely fit in any environment, you can effortlessly collaborate with others and achieve what you want from them. Without social skills, your growth will be significantly slowed, and all your interactions will be ineffective. Selfish, ignorant, socially disconnected, and highly opinionated people lack social awareness.

If you are not comfortable with people, changes, and policies in a professional setting, you will always feel unfit and never accomplish anything. Our ego, inferiority complex, and prejudice will shape our social consciousness. It means being kind to everyone and everything around us. We must not think of ourselves as superior to others. We must always consider how our actions will affect others. When our social awareness improves, we will develop a service-oriented mindset.

We should always be empathetic toward others. Kindness must permeate all our acts. Many people confuse empathy with favouritism. Once, a manager told me having empathy is the same as favouring people. Not at all. Empathy doesn't mean you'll treat your employees better. Instead, it's a tool that helps you understand how your decisions affect others.

Empathy is the ability to sense other people's emotions, coupled with the ability to imagine what someone else might be thinking or feeling. As per studies, there are two types of empathy: affective empathy and cognitive empathy.

Affective empathy refers to the sensations and feelings we get in response to others' emotions. It is just that we feel stressed when we detect others' feelings. But cognitive empathy is when we can identify and understand others' feelings. Leaders devoid of cognitive empathy will never be able to motivate their teams to realize their full potential. The day you develop empathy is the day when your life will begin to transform.

Being socially aware will help us get along with other people, get them to work together, and lead employees toward a common goal.

Every day, you may encounter a lot of disagreements. The people who can manage conflict keep turnover low and productivity high. Our ability to foster strong morale, ease stress in the workplace, clear up any misunderstandings, and improve communication all hinges on how well our employees interact with one another. It's not just for your employees; it's also for your customers, suppliers, and vendors, who are part of your business.

In a broad sense, it refers to having awareness and comprehension of the world as it is. This includes environments, cultures, societal norms, problems, and struggles that make up the social atmosphere in which we live.

Treat others the way you want to be treated. To enhance our social skills, we must develop our soft skills.

Relationship management:

Professional relationships are about being friends with a purpose. If a manager dislike any of his employees, he will soon find a reason to fire them. If an employee doesn't like the management, he will soon find a reason to quit. In business, this is normal. A manager will never find someone who is an exact copy of the person he or she wants to work with. Similarly, an employee is unlikely to find their ideal boss. It will go on forever until we learn how to keep relationships going. If you can't keep a good relationship with your employees and customers, they will find another good company to work for.

A 75-year-old, the longest of any research ever conducted, has proven that not money, fame, status, or wealth makes a man happy and healthy, but a positive relationship with everyone.

From the time we are born, we start making connections with everyone. You will be happier and more accomplished if you have good relationships with everyone and everything in your life.

Imagine a day when you feel nothing but happy for everyone you come into contact with. Will your life ever be depressing? However, each connection establishes a boundary. You'd be wise not to breach that threshold, dubbed their "private zone," if you want to maintain a healthy relationship for the long term.

A manager who refuses to listen to any of his employees can result in daily mess-ups. In such an environment, everyone will work with fear, and workers will conceal their problems. If a manager does not acknowledge the frustration and anger of his workers, it is difficult to establish a healthy relationship with them.

Emotional intelligence is the capacity to make your people adopt change and grow to the company's requirements. To establish a solid connection, frequently express gratitude to your employees, colleagues, and customers for their efforts rather than their results.

The best relationship advice I can offer is not to have any expectations of others. The expectation will establish a degree of hope. When hope is shattered, we feel dreadful. You will have a hard time keeping the balance in that relationship.

Reading others' moods and thoughts and making strong connections with them is a great art and skill. Respect, transparency, humility, and clarity are fundamental to developing a good relationship.

Always find a solution where both parties can win for the same reason. If you want to get an extra five hours of work from an employee, apart from giving overtime money, give an extra day off if required or provide a nice family dine-out option.

Cut down on gossip and politics. Treat everyone equally. Be an optimist. The best aspect of optimism is it ensures we'll keep trying, no matter what happens. Optimism gives you the conviction that, if you are willing to work through any challenging circumstances with a positive outlook, they will all pass without any difficulties.

More than 100 managers of Fortune 500 companies have been studied to know the impact of emotional intelligence on their leadership. Those with good emotional intelligence had higher sensitivity and empathy and were more expressive. They were rated the most influential leaders. They received higher merit and performance ratings.

Our brains change throughout our lives. So, it can mold it for the better when we practice emotional intelligence. Our childhood is the best time to learn and practice emotional intelligence. Childhood depression, abuse, and other disorders all affect our emotional awareness. Research shows that if you want your child to have a better life, you should help them develop their emotional intelligence.

Low emotional intelligence people are always argumentative; they do not listen to anyone, blame others for every problem, are full of complaints, have poor mental health, and have emotional outbursts. Our mental health is a reflection of how we deal with emotions. Persons who are completely complaint-free are either (a) undergoing profound inner transformation or (b) knowing growth is not an outcome of complaining, but rather rising beyond it.

Teams with high emotional intelligence have faster cohesion, work more efficiently in a short period, are happy with their team's communication, and have greater social support from one another. Good EI is associated with a fulfilling social and family life, improved academic achievement, and better physical and mental health.

It is a continuous practice and a conscious choice to become an emotionally intelligent person.

Have you ever seen a great leader who is perpetually angry? No way.

Have you ever seen a great leader who is not receptive to others? No way.

Have you ever seen a great leader whose decisions are always catastrophic? No way.

Have you ever seen a great leader become a problem for the company? No way.

Have you ever seen a great leader whose presence irritates co-workers? No way.

Have you ever seen a great leader who is constantly blaming others for failures? No way.

Have you ever seen a great leader who is incapable of running a company? No way.

Though we all know this to be true, why don't we succeed, and why do we waste practically all our time in despair and grumbling? You hold the answer within you. You are the source of your happiness and your sorrow. Go deeper within yourself till you discover your own spirit. It is sentient and transcendent of rules and regulations. Ask questions until you get the answers you need. All of your conditioning, insecurities, beliefs, and fears will disappear in a moment. All you need is time to get to know yourselves better than you actually do.

Motivation: Pushes to The Extreme

If the sole reason for you to start a business is to make money, you probably won't succeed. The goal of a business is not to make money. Money is the reflection of the value we create, and profit is the compound effect of that value. You can't inspire your employees and customers if you do not have a higher purpose than a materialistic attitude.

Successful people have one thing in common: They wake up every day with a clear goal; if we can figure out that one thing in our lives, we won't need any outside stimulation. To get things done, we need something to "push" us. We can't reach our full potential with the help of money, people, jobs, things, or status; we need a reason that pushes us out of our comfort zone. There should be a reason why we're different from everyone else. A reason that defines our strength. A purpose we can be proud of.

Many of us do not know what it means to push ourselves. Have you ever heard the saying, "shoot for the moon; even if you miss, you will land among the stars"? This encourages us to strive for excellence because even if we fail, we will still be on top of those who don't even try. That is what it means to push yourself.

The story of a Kasturi Hiran (musk deer) in the Upanishad is very famous. When she was a kid, she began to notice a pleasant scent coming from somewhere. She went out to find where this smell was coming from. She went deep into the forest, smelled every tree, swam in the water, and climbed every hill and mountain.

She spent all her life looking for the smell, but she never found it. One day, like any other day, she was searching for the scent on top of a hill when she slipped and hurt herself very badly. While lying on the ground, gravely hurt, she realized that the scent she was seeking had always emanated from her own body. What we're looking for is already inside of us. We do not have to wait for external incentives to make changes in our lives.

Somehow, we got it in our heads that listening to the achievements of others would inspire us to work harder. The outside stimulation gives an instant spark to your feelings, nothing else. There's no way it could motivate you permanently. We would not have gotten our independence in 1947 if Mahatma Gandhi had to wait for someone to motivate him.

Mahatma Gandhi never fought for the freedom of oppressed people in our country. Instead, he fought for the truth and chose the path of Ahimsa (nonviolence). This is how he was different from the other freedom fighters. He didn't hate the British people, which is why he succeeded. The other revolutionaries, on the other hand, hated the British and chose violence to win. There is never any success at the end of a violent act.

Motivation is an action, not a goal. Only your efforts are appreciated, not your results. According to my research, three factors are essential to be motivated in life: **goodness of heart, originality, and the value of effort.** When you have a good heart, your actions become unique, and unique actions will deliver the greatest value. The rest are motivated by fame, pleasure, comfort, status, and money. This is why we shaped our lives with a more materialistic outlook than a realistic one.

I never met a person who was motivated without goodness in their heart. I never met a person who was motivated without being original in their actions. I've never met a person who was motivated by trivial matters.

The goodness of the heart is a prerequisite for self-motivation. If you lack goodness, it doesn't matter how big your task or dream is, you will never be motivated. You will never aim to make something of the highest value.

Take any historical figure, whether it is Abraham Lincoln, Nikola Tesla, or Swamy Vivekananda; they all upheld goodness throughout their lives, whether it was constitutional, technological, spiritual, or cultural. They all fought for one thing, value. They have worked so hard to deliver the greatest value possible, hoping that the world will benefit from their efforts.

An action is always neutral; it is not good or bad. Motive is what makes an action right or wrong. Those who have no regard for goodness will be motivated by the wrong values. This will only bring more destructive thoughts.

Michael Swango was an American physician. He was one of the most notorious serial killers in history. He poisoned about sixty patients to death. Since he was three years old, he had been very interested in murders and violent deaths. Sadistic pleasures motivated him throughout his childhood. He kept a journal detailing murders. He was totally obsessed with the Holocaust. He secretly kept photos of crimes and death camps. He was later found guilty and sentenced to three life terms in jail.

To be motivated, we must carry goodness in our hearts; otherwise, negative thoughts will lead our entire life. Negative influences will prevent you from ever becoming self-motivated. Our beliefs and value systems play a crucial role for a good heart.

Corruption, power conflict, fraud, discrimination, crimes, and a plethora of superstitious beliefs like black magic, animal sacrifices, etc., will continue to plague our society if we lack goodness. Nothing good can come from a bad environment. It is now a scientific fact and not a philosophical statement anymore. When you practice goodness in your workplace, you are elevating the spirit of your workforce.

When we live by high moral standards, we naturally become good. To make your heart lighter, you must rid yourself of all your burdens. We carry around unnecessary loads from the past, which makes our hearts beat faster. When we have goodness in our hearts, we tend to respect people and help them. There will be changes in our character, and we will become more compassionate and empathetic. We shall extend forgiveness and maintain a vibrant spirit. We will become more human in nature. We enjoy every moment and don't curse destiny. We do not believe in fate and wish to build our own fate.

Long-term success requires establishing credibility with your audience, and for that, you need to earn their trust and confidence. When you are original, you will undoubtedly stand out from the crowd.

Without being original in our actions, we cannot justify our lives. Originality is the surest way to gain others' long-term confidence. It is the only way to distinguish oneself from others. Anyone, who has lied about who they are, can be easily identified.

People often adopt a false persona, hoping that others will accept them. In the long run, this approach will fail. Those who compromise their authenticity will never be accepted in the real world. Original people are the only ones who can devote one hundred percent to any task. The original people set realistic goals and take the right actions. They never settle for an average life. They are also satisfied workers and are more likely to meet deadlines.

Ever wonder why some people consistently fall short of expectations despite receiving extensive training and coaching? The reason is that they aren't original. Their plan is not to work hard but rather to involve in something else. Ninety-nine percent of workers are not original in their actions. All of them are just trying to impress their boss. Instead we should try to impress ourselves, so we are ready to face any problems head-on at work.

We all want to be perceived as more intelligent, smart, honest, wealthy, powerful, and fearless than others. However, this is all fake. This will have a negative impact on our originality. Internally motivated people put in more effort than others. High performance is the result of internal motivation. We have moved from a knowledge-based economy to a skill-based economy. Motivation is much needed in today's workplace.

Many of us may wonder how to develop originality. The one way you can improve your originality is by being curious. Curiosity brings originality. When you are curious, you have the tendency to know things better and deeper. It fuels motivation. Try to be curious about every topic that interests you.

There is a way for us to cultivate curiosity. Try to learn the history of everything you see. For example, the next time you eat Lays, try to find out how potato chips came to be. The first time anyone heard about potato chips was in 1853 in Santiago Springs, New York, when a frustrated cook George Crum was trying to please a demanding customer. The customer was unhappy because the fried potato was too thick to eat. He returned it twice to the kitchen. The irritated chef sliced potatoes thinly, fried them until they were crisp, and seasoned them with salt, so the customer would find them inedible. But it came as a surprise that he really liked the dish. This is how potato chips were invented. Make an effort to learn the history of everything you encounter to become more curious.

Many stories from our country have inspired us all. The efforts of a single person can change the course of history. When I first went to an ISKON temple near my home, I met a monk there, Lakshman Dasa. He taught me many things about spirituality with clarity. But the history of ISKON Temple is worth knowing.

The question is, "What do we do when we're in our seventies?" We enter our most vulnerable phase of life. We want to relax as much as possible, as we believe these are our final days. We will fear taking on any sort of responsibility. This doesn't work for great people, though.

Abhay Charanaravinda Bhakti Vedanta Swamy Srila Prabhupada was a monk who left India for the United States when he was in his seventies. He had one goal: to bring ancient Indian wisdom to the rest of the world. He travelled on a cargo ship and took thirty-seven days to reach New York. He had two severe heart attacks along the way. Without much money, he arrived in New York City. He knew no one there. He was confused about what to do next and where to start. But he started his mission without any delay. He began preaching the Bhagavad-Gita on the streets of America.

In America, things were quite challenging at that time. After World War II, Americans were going through a cultural change with the rise of the hippie movement. Srila Prabhupada suffered many terrible things on the streets of America. His only belongings, his books and typewriter, were stolen one day. After facing many difficulties in his very old age, he kept trying. He kept doing what he had to do, and in the end, he became the most revered spiritual teacher of all time.

He travelled around the world fifteen times during the 1960s and '70s. He penned over ten thousand letters to his disciples around the world. He built over a hundred temples, cultural centres, and ashrams in many different places worldwide. He translated many of the ancient Sanskrit books, like the Bhagavad-Gita and Bhagavatam, into English and many other languages. He used to work twenty-two hours a day.

He authored over 70 volumes on the Krishna tradition. More than five thousand disciples were formally inducted by him. To help the temples financially, he founded an incense business. He came up with the idea of the free meal program, which now feeds millions of poor people. He started Bhakti Vedanta Book Trust to publish his book and countless other things.

Can you imagine all these accomplishments he achieved in a total of twelve years, from 1965 to 1977? No force can impede a self-motivated person. They live and work like superhumans. This is the power of goodness in the heart, originality in actions, and value of effort. If you follow this path, you will never lack motivation until the day you die.

Every manager always wants to know how to get their team going. But the point is no one can motivate a person who isn't self-motivated and who doesn't have any interests or goals in life.

If you can understand human psychology, you can motivate your employees to some extent. Human behaviour is purposeful and motivated by the need for satisfaction. Human needs can never be satisfied. Needs can be classified according to their hierarchical importance, from the lowest to the highest. There are five recognized human needs: psychological, safety, love, self-esteem, and self-actualization, according to Maslow's hierarchy of needs.

The first human need is psychological. It is the most basic human need. These include food, water, shelter, and clothes. When our psychological needs are not met, it is difficult to meet the following need, which is the safety need.

The second human need after psychological needs is safety. It is about protection, emotional well-being, health, and financial security.

After the safety needs, our third need is love. This is physical and emotional intimacy, bonding with friends and family.

The fourth is the need for self-esteem. This is driven by self-respect. It can be based on respect and acknowledgement from others and self-assessment.

Fifth and final on Maslow's hierarchy, self-actualization is at the pinnacle of the human experience. It is the fulfilment of our true potential. Even if we try very hard, this path is hard to reach in a lifetime.

Today, almost every employee is satisfied with their first level of psychological needs. If you can help them achieve other human needs, such as safety and self-esteem, you can motivate your employees to some extent.

Encourage your workers to upskill with the knowledge they have. Encourage them to have a goal in their life. Teach them how to save money to become more financially independent. Give them feedback frequently. This will help them achieve their personal and professional goals. Create a culture designed for asking questions, not working with a fixed mindset. This will ignite the inner drive.

A British psychologist studied how animals reacted to rewards. Surprisingly, those who receive food after each training session perform far better than those who do not. Similarly, various neuroscientific studies have been conducted on how our brain responds to rewards. If you thank your employees sincerely for their effort, most of them will do even better the next time. Here, expressing gratitude to your employees won't cost you anything.

A study conducted on workers in the United States found that recognition and appreciation boost productivity by 40%. You can motivate your employees by giving them the authority to make decisions and correct their actions from time to time, and also the freedom to try new things.

On the other hand, many managers granted positions to their employees but not independence or authority. In many companies, I have seen there are many supervisors, in-charge persons, and senior executives, but none of them has decision-making authority. Positions have little to do with productivity; instead, they will corrupt people. We should assign positions to promote a strong work ethic, not just for the roles' sake.

Motivation will fluctuate until you follow the right method. When I started writing this book, I thought I could start a business that could help small-scale businesses. Later, I was motivated by the fame that I could get from it if my book became a best seller. But after a while, I thought that my parents would be very proud of me if I did something good.

But what truly motivated me was the realization that those who read my book will evaluate my capabilities based on the quality of my content. Therefore, I strive harder each day to produce the best writing possible so that every reader will appreciate my efforts. This was the real motivation; the rest only stayed with me for a very short time.

Our attention is constantly diverted. Our lives aren't meant to be boring or useless. But the problem is we want to do many things at once and try to be good at everything, which we can't. The problem is not with the Internet or technology, but with the way we think. We want to be artists today, singers tomorrow, YouTubers tomorrow, actors tomorrow, teachers tomorrow, public speakers the next day, and so on. The difficulty, though, is we do not consider what is within our competency.

The quality of your circumstances improves when the quality of your thoughts improves. We are not so self-motivated because we have a lot of free time, have no passion for anything, are not involved in anything creative in life, are under constant stress, or we are good procrastinators. Our total involvement in life and work is limited. This is why we are not self-motivated.

Say to yourself first thing in the morning, today I am healthy; my mind is peaceful. No matter how many difficulties I face, I will try my best. I'll prove I'm a good person. I don't want to look back on the day with regret. I will spend the day in the present without worrying about the past or the future. I will not allow anyone or anything negative to influence my emotions. I won't waste my time doing useless things. I will work on my strengths and my passion. I will never let anyone complain about my character. I will never let anyone get hurt because of me, whether it's physically, mentally, or emotionally. Today, I will help someone in need. I will do the work as if it were my final day on earth. I will do my job without thinking about the result.

This is not just something you say; you should follow it. This will, without a doubt, will change your life for the better.

If you are not motivated by far, do not worry; focus on the job in hand. Whatever you are doing now, the more effort you put in, the more you will value it.

In 2011, for a study, a group of people split into two groups. One group was told to look at the Ikea furniture, while the other group was told to assemble the furniture. After that, they were asked how much they were willing to pay for the furniture. The group that assembled the furniture was ready to pay 63% more than the first group who just looked at the furniture. If we put more effort into something, we value it more. This is called the Ikea effect, where more labour leads to love.

The science behind motivation is that when we do certain things, we get a rush of dopamine, which makes us feel good right away. Neuroscientists conducted experiments on mice and discovered that the more dopamine the mice had, the higher the barrier they could climb to get food compared to mice with less or no dopamine.

When you have goodness in your heart and originality in your actions, and you think about the value of your efforts, you don't need to worry about your dopamine levels; they will rise organically.

Kaizen: Daily Navigator Tool

Progress lies in improvements in daily activity. We don't focus on improvement when busy with our daily tasks. You will make real progress when you seek the difference between the circumstances where you are now and where you want to be.

Kaizen is a Japanese word that signifies change for the better. After the Second World War, the Japanese economy was severely damaged. All major cities, industries, transportation, and morale across the country have been severely impacted. A serious food scarcity persisted for several years. The "occupation of Japan" (to revive the economy) by the Allied powers began in 1945 and concluded in 1952. US quality experts and business gurus performed the entire process. The economy began to rise slowly, but the level of success achieved over the years was outstanding. Even US companies were threatened by the quality of Japanese products.

In the years following World War II, American auto executives visited Japanese Toyota car factories to find out how they built world-class cars without major quality issues. They found a philosophy called Kaizen, which motivated them to produce excellent products. They learned that at Toyota's factory, instead of punishing workers for making mistakes, Toyota has asked workers to make suggestions when a problem arises. This human-centred approach is now widely known as Kaizen.

Kaizen is a Japanese term that became popular after the Japanese product quality, but it all started in the United States during World War II." Training Within Industries" was the practice of giving suggestions to improve productivity by everyone working in a company to support US soldiers and their allies on the war field to reach the arms and ammunition and other equipment on time. As a result, productivity, quality, and timely delivery have increased.

If you are a shortcut guy (searching for a shortcut solution), then this title is not for you. Success cannot be attained in a single great leap; instead, it is the constant effort of small steps taken together, called marginal gains. There are three aspects to the concept of Kaizen. It is working with people who can contribute to growth, making marginal improvements to get where you want to go, and finally, creating a system that reduces the chances of error. The beauty of Kaizen is that it can be implemented at a low or no cost.

Nowadays, not only Japanese companies but almost all companies worldwide practice kaizen as a daily routine. Big companies such as Toyota, Nestlé, and Canon use Kaizen as a key component of their business models. Lockheed Martin, an American security and aerospace company, has incorporated kaizen into its hardware management to reduce manufacturing costs, inventory, and delivery time. There are many more examples and success stories, even in the small business setup.

The basis of Kaizen in one manufacturing facility is,

Housekeeping; as a rule of thumb, introducing good housekeeping will reduce the failure rate by 50%, and employees will maintain cleanliness and discipline.

Waste elimination; suppose that a company adds 5 Muda to the value of each part; then the productivity can be doubled by reducing Muda and increasing the value-added to two parts.

Standardization; standards are the most effective ways to do the work. The best work ethic is the best standard.

Kaizen has two major functions in any company: maintenance and improvement. Maintenance consists of taking appropriate measures in the case of bottlenecks, whether technological, management, or other operational standards. Improvements are activities aimed at enhancing existing systems and standards for better work culture.

Most managers today find it hard to maintain growth for a long time. When we recommend the Kaizen method to get out of this situation, most managers always say the same thing: We need a quick fix. We didn't have time to sit around and wait for the results. So, to fix the problems quickly, employees, plans, policies, and so on are always being changed. It's just going to make things worse.

If a quick fix were the best way to go, then our country wouldn't have been struggling for 50 years to get independence, Japan would have gotten over the effects of the world war in a few days, and technology would have changed in a matter of seconds. But likewise, it never happened because a quick fix is not a solution but a bad practice.

Because most of the time, we are preoccupied with secondary situations and assume that they may be solved quickly. In a company, there are two situations: primary and secondary. We lose control of everything when we focus on secondary information. If we are able to focus on the primary situation, we can solve any problem.

For example, a secondary situation statement is that employees do not respect me. The primary situation, though, is to repair the culture and focus on training people.

A secondary situation statement is that my quality isn't up to par. But the key statement should be something like, "My quality-control system is inadequate."

A secondary situation statement is, "My employees are not listening to me" or "I can't handle my people". The primary situation statement is that you lack many skills needed to manage your employees.

Most managers pay attention to information that isn't as primary, like the number of machine breakdowns, the rate of quality rejections, a lack of work ethic, morality, work standardization, unhappy customers, delivery problems, or the hygiene of the workplace. They focus on secondary information and keep pointing fingers at everyone else. When it moves past a safe point, it becomes hard to understand the primary information.

Focusing on secondary information is always more comfortable because it is an easy method to blame others rather than fix the root cause.

The story of the British bicycle team is the best example of Kaizen. The cycling team in Britain had only won one gold medal in the history of 76 years. Professional cyclists in Great Britain have endured nearly a hundred years of mediocrity. In 2002, the Board of Directors for Professional cycling in Britain hired Dave Brailsford as their new director of performance. The performance of British riders had been so poor that one of Europe's top bike manufacturers refused to sell bikes to the team for fear of damaging sales if other professionals saw the Brits using their gear.

Brailsford was hired to take British cycling to the next level. He focused on small changes, which is called the "aggregation of marginal gains." He redesigned the motorcycle seats to make them more comfortable and rubbed alcohol on the tyres for better traction. He asked runners to wear electrically heated shorts to maintain a perfect muscle temperature while climbing and used biofeedback sensors to monitor how each athlete responded to a particular workout. The team put different fabrics through tests in a wind tunnel and then told their outdoor runners to switch to indoor racing suits, which turned out to be lighter and better at cutting through the air.

But that's not all he did. Brailsford and his team continued to find 1% improvements in unexpected areas. They tested different types of massage gels to see which one led to the most rapid muscle recovery. They hired a surgeon to teach each rider how to wash their hands best to reduce the chances of getting a cold. They researched which type of pillow and mattress led to the best night's sleep for each runner. They even painted the inside of the team truck white, which helped them spot little bits of dust that would normally slip by unnoticed but could degrade the performance of the finely tuned bikes.

Hundreds of these tiny improvements accumulated, and the result was overwhelming. Just five years after Brailsford took over, the British Cycling team dominated the road and track cycling events at the 2008 Olympic Games in Beijing, where they won an astounding 60 percent of the gold medals. Four years later, when the Olympic Games came to London, the British raised the bar by setting nine Olympic records and seven world records.

In the same year, Bradley Wiggins became the first British rider to win the Tour de France. The next year, his teammate, Chris Froome, won the race, and he would go on to win repeatedly in 2015, 2016, and 2017, giving the British team five Tour de France victories in six years.

From 2007 to 2017, British cyclists won 178 world championships and 66 Olympic or Paralympic gold medals; they captured five Tour de France victories in what is widely regarded as the most successful run-in cycling history. It represents the real power of marginal gains. It is one of the best examples of successful Kaizen.

Kaizen is difficult, but it appears because it is a people-centred philosophy. You cannot benefit from kaizen if there is no teamwork, a good system, a standard of work, or good leadership.

It is a thought process rather than an innovative approach. Also, it is a never-ending process, with the involvement of everyone. It is very different from innovation or a short-term vision. Innovation is a big leap. Innovation needs more capital, more resources, more data, new technology, a dedicated workforce, extra focus, and market research. What if your innovation fails to achieve the desired results? You wasted all your efforts with no actual use.

If you practice Kaizen at its best in your organization, it will improve productivity, competence, and profitability.

Before starting a Kaizen journey, always ask these three questions,

- What does long-term success in a particular area look like, and what should be my priorities to achieve that?

- What is the smallest yet most effective step that I can take every day? How can I identify that my 20% activity produces 80% results?

- Who can be my mentor, teacher, and partner for this venture? Is there anyone else who can support me, and is there any new technology to help me get what I want?

Ask these questions to start a Kaizen journey, and use a journal to track your daily progress. Ask this question every day: Did I walk on the correct path, or do I need to change my direction further?

A thousand-mile journey begins with a single step. Consistency is the key to becoming indispensable. What is even more wonderful about a Kaizen journey is that you will develop strong willpower, a positive attitude, a good focus, and perseverance; these all are important elements to becoming more successful. Instant improvement will create confusion, but small continuous improvement brings clarity to the process.

If we can measure, we can make improvements at any event. The compound effect is the backbone of any business. If any process you are doing is not done well, its value will diminish over time. It doesn't need more capital or great people; it just needs good plans and actions. Being consistent is the key to outperforming. If you think you are underperforming, the best thing you can do is to push yourself to work harder than usual.

Many companies stop improving after they notice progress somewhere. It is like celebrating victory before it occurs. They assume they are moving in the right direction. Don't stop making improvements just because you're getting good results. You'll end up where you started if you do so. Instead, take process improvement to a new level. Leave those who aren't improving; they are the obstacles to the way of any growth. It is okay to fire anyone, regardless of the position, if they are not adding any value.

Kaizen can be implemented not just in business but in our personal lives too. Everyone should practice Kaizen in their personal lives so that they can become a better version of themselves. For example, you don't need to go to Harvard or start a company if you want to retire with a million dollars. You just need to invest a small amount each month, and you will be a millionaire in retirement.

Solving the problem may not necessarily help you to become successful, but upgrading the situation will. If you adhere to the rules, Kaizen will undoubtedly upgrade your company.

I curated the below illustration from the book Atomic Habits. You can follow the instructions below to get a clear picture of your margin gains.

I've created a model that will help you comprehend the value of Kaizen in your personal and professional life.

Included mathematical illustrations to facilitate your understanding.

If you spend 1% every day to improve any of your skills, you become so good when you reach the 463rd day. Let's look at how it could work.

Start from where you are, and do it consistently without fail.

The power of 1% in life; Daily improvement:

1% daily increment = 1+.01= 1.01%

10th day – 1.01^{10} = 1.10% increment (the tiniest increment on the tenth day, you can't even feel that you are moving towards progress)

50th day – 1.01^{50} = 1.644% increment (If somebody is so consistent up to the 50th day, even become confused about progress)

100th day – 1.01^{100} = 2.70% increment (can you still believe you are on the right track??)

150th day – 1.01^{150} = 4.44% increment (you shall doubt yourself and most probably plan to quit)

200th day – 1.01^{200} = 7.31% increment (decided to quit, no sign of improving even after a constant effort)

250th day – 1.01^{250} = 12.03% increment (those who are still not given up can see a bit of hope)

300th day – 1.01^{300} = 19.78% increment (happy that progress is now visible)

365th day (one year) – 1.01^{365} = 37.783% increment (now you can confidently work on a specific skill that you have been practicing for over a year, a great sign of hope)

400th day – 1.01^{400} = 53% increment (wow!!! This is huge development)

450th day – 1.01^{450} = 88% (Haha… Now you are a master)

462nd day – 1.01^{462} = 99.19% (unbeatable, keep moving, you have nailed it!!! It is the beauty of consistency and perseverance).

Daily reduction:

If you don't spend enough time improving your skills, you will lose your ability to use the skill in less than 100 days. Shocking information, right? Look at the mathematical data given below.

If you don't improve yourself today, you are stuck in your yesterday.

1% daily reduction = 1-.01= .99%

10th day - $.99^{10}$ = 90.4% (the tiniest decrease, you can't feel the danger ahead)

30th day - $.99^{30}$ = 73.9% (still hard to recognize the downfall, but there will be symptoms like increasing laziness)

50th day - $.99^{50}$ = 60.5% (you start feeling an unprecedented resistance in learning, and you feel lethargic almost all the time. The danger zone is nearby)

70th day - $.99^{70}$ = 49.4% (This could be the point where the return to normalcy becomes so hard, your energy level becomes so low)

100th day - $.99^{100}$ = 36.6% (you are now in the danger zone, it took 500 days of hard work to reach the same percentage of increment, but you have wasted your precious time)

135th day - $.99^{135}$ = 25.7% (reluctance to work hard, can't attract luck or produce good opportunity)

180th day - $.99^{180}$ = 16.3% (addicted, lost, and angry you become, the freshness of life will be lost completely, we don't need to calculate furthermore).

365th day - $.99^{365}$ = 3% (back to square 1, completely wasted a year in your life).

Time Management: The Most Sensible Tool

Do you write your daily schedule on a calendar? Do you plan out everything for your business? How disciplined is your daily routine? Can you write down how much you've accomplished by the end of the day? If your response is "no," then you're probably just wondering about your job. You must, without a doubt, educate yourself on the rules of efficient time management.

Seeing things from different perspectives helps us understand the value of time. Ask a person how much a second is worth if they ever lost an Olympic gold medal in a fraction of a second. The value of a minute can be explained when scoring a winning goal in the last minute of a soccer match. We will recognize the value of an hour when we overcook our breakfast or get stuck in traffic. When we miss a significant event in our lives, we know the value of a day. A year after failing a university exam, we will understand the value of a year. We'll know how precious our life is when we're old and grey.

For centuries, scientists have pondered the question of how to define time. No one really succeeded in defining what time is; Einstein was the most successful in this regard. In physics, space and time are related. Space is considered three-dimensional, and the addition of time makes our world four-dimensional. Due to the fact that everything is relative to time, time is the essence of everything if we have to succeed in our four-dimensional environment.

Life is full of possibilities if we value every minute of it. Everything else can be replaced at some point. In this world, those, who value time, have limitless opportunities. Those who waste their time miss out on all genuine opportunities. This is the reason why time-wasters seek shortcuts in life.

In today's world, the right opportunities are key to success. As soon as we convince ourselves we have enough time to do a task, we consider putting it off and diminishing its significance. A person who puts things off never gets anything worthwhile in life.

During my research, I noticed one thing in common: almost everyone in the company arrives on time in the morning and leaves very late. When I asked, they said they hadn't finished the work to go home on time. Many of the employees grumbled about the same thing: their time. They are unable to finish the work on time. Every day at work, they are confused and stressed.

This could be because they work too much, don't know how to manage their time, or don't know what they are doing with their work. Most of the time, it's clear that they haven't managed their time well.

We all want to get the work done as quickly as possible. Because of poor time management, we delayed almost every work that could have been avoided. We all have twenty-four hours a day; however, some people find it extremely easy to accomplish the task, while others find it quite difficult.

To become more productive at work, to become more relaxed at work, and add more value to your company, you must master time management. There are several rules that, if you follow them in your daily life, I will guarantee you never experience unnecessary delays at work. To make our lives organized, we need to follow certain laws and rules of nature. Because the way time works depends on how disciplined you are in your daily life.

1st rule: Learning from our own and others' mistakes is the golden guideline for freeing up more time in our schedules. If we repeat the same mistake, it indicates we haven't learned anything from it. Don't allow your employees to make the same mistake that has previously occurred in your company. If you ignore the mistake, it will happen again, but this time the impact may be many times higher than the first time. Now you are not saving time for your company's future. Your time is spent dealing with everyday issues.

No one can reverse time. In hindsight, you may regret your mistakes, thinking they could have been avoided. The more time you invest in preventing errors, the less time you'll save to do the important work. Our time will be more valuable in the future if we learn things faster than other people.

The time is moving forward. Thinking about your achievements from yesterday will get you nothing today or tomorrow.

2nd rule: When you understand the important things and focus on them, you may liberate yourself from a multitude of distractions. When you focus on the right task, you can get much more done than taking action on unnecessary activities. The theory of time dictates that we should decide what we want to do and devote definite time to it. We can accomplish any superhuman task if we know what must be done right now because time controls the process, not the result. But we are obsessed with results and have no time to improve the process.

3rd rule: How we can achieve more in less. Apply this rule. Time works for you based on how effectively your schedule aligns with company requirements. Any task must take enough time to finish it. However, by applying our talent, expertise, intellect, and teamwork, we can increase the pace of work and finish it in less time.

Use technology to plan your day. We can get rid of many routine tasks with the help of technology. Many software tools can help you save time and get more done. Today, it is considerably more affordable. What we need is the right mindset to use these technologies. Find the most suitable technology to enhance the effort.

4th rule: How do you eat the elephant in the room? Little by little, right? We must learn to work in batches to be more efficient. From morning to evening, divide your time into manageable segments. Don't count the time in quarters, months, or years, but in minutes. The more we count in minutes, the more value adds up over time.

Set up each task into two groups: important and urgent. Plan everything important and do it first thing in the morning. Planning and preparation eliminate all the unproductive tasks in a process.

We may view this idea from a different angle. How can we eat an elephant quickly? We can divide it equally among everyone. That's the course of action we ought to take —an equal share of the work for each person. If everyone gets an equal share based on their skill and experience level, we can certainly eat an elephant very quickly.

5th rule: Time is money. It is true because saving time in the workplace will save money. If you want to save money, you should consider ways to save time. When you save time on labour, you save on costs. For example, if the cycle time of your product is 5 minutes (which is just an example) and you have 1440 minutes of working in a day (3 shifts), every day, you can manufacture 288 parts. Think about how you could save one minute per part. After saving one minute, you can now make 360 parts in a day, which is a 25% increase. This will only reflect on your bottom line when you cut down on work hours and the payroll changes because of it.

6th rule: The art of delegation is the key to saving your valuable time. A manager must know how to delegate all the tasks effectively. Make sure the people you're assigning work must know what exactly you expect from them. If you pass only half the information, it will produce nothing. Delegation is when you give away some of your important work; if you do not give the exact details and do not ask for feedback on time, the delegated work will never be completed. Any skill you find hard to implement in your company, delegate it.

As per a study, a manager who delegated responsibility efficiently generated 33% higher revenue.

7th rule: Stop procrastinating. Build a culture where problems are solved right away. You can procrastinate the work by valuing it from a lower one to a higher one. Understanding the higher intensity of work could mean solving customer complaints, finding the root cause of a recurring issue, or improving the system and standards. Lower-intensity tasks, such as sending emails and speaking with a new supplier, as well as meetings, phone calls, and office distractions, are all time wasters.

8th rule: The Pareto Principle and Parkinson's Law are two powerful concepts in time management. The Pareto Principle directs our attention to the few most important activities. Parkinson's Law states that work expands to occupy the time available to complete it. This means that if you give someone ten hours to do something, it takes ten hours to do it. But if you give five hours to do the same task, it will only take five hours to finish it.

9th rule: Time management doesn't mean that we should manage our time; it means we should manage our priorities. The Ola electric two-wheeler factory in India recently announced that they would manufacture 5,500 bikes a day. The priority at the Ola plant is to produce as many vehicles as possible in record time to make their models difficult for others to imitate.

This strategy will reduce waiting time, ensure quick delivery, and increase customer satisfaction. They spend their money on robotics, process automation, artificial intelligence technologies, and, of course, the best time management ideas so that their priorities will meet the requirements. If you understand the logic behind setting priorities, navigating your daily life will be a lot less of a challenge for you.

Priorities are the backbone of effective time management. Your priorities are oblivious to others in your company, which is why your time management is ineffective. We should have clarity on what the company stands for, what a customer is looking for, how we can bring more value to everyone associated with us, and how we can move forward faster than the competition.

For example, if your goal is to outperform Usain Bolt in a 100-meter sprint, you probably won't succeed. But if you make it a priority to run as quickly as you can and give it your best, you might get good results. This is the hidden power of setting priorities.

10th rule: Be relevant all the time. You can't build value on the first day, the second day, or the 1000th day if you are not relevant. Your relevancy builds power. Legacy does not do any justice to your company if you're not relevant anymore. Be relevant in terms of technology, expertise, workforce, methodology, and beliefs.

Things are constantly evolving. We must always be ready for what comes next. But if we stay stuck in the past, we lose both today and tomorrow. "The early bird gets the worm" is a famous idiom. It only matters how much you're ahead of your competition.

A hundred years ago, if someone told you it was possible to land on the moon with the help of a machine, would you believe that? Today, if anyone talks about the moon landing, you don't doubt them. The value of time will always change with reference to external factors. Great leaders have insights to see the external factors way before they come. Therefore, they are well-prepared and impervious to failure. Great leaders always try to stay up-to-date and plan for the future simultaneously.

Reflect on your past. If you continue to work the way you do, it will cost you effort, but it won't bring any positive change. It is easy to find out how many hours we have wasted in a day. Fortunately, these are the events that we have control over if you can reflect them on your day.

11th rule: The best time for hammering iron is when it is very hot. No matter how hard you try, if the iron isn't hot enough, all your effort will be for nothing. Time and proper effort are where the result comes from. Before managing time, we have to know when the best time is to do something. During my research, I saw that many companies started improvement initiatives quite late. Due to the fact that it is already so late, it is difficult to predict how much effort will be required to effect change. So, most of the companies eventually gave up on their projects, which is sad.

12th rule: Ramu and Raju are friends. They're both employed. After work, Ramu liked to party. At the same time, Raju took time to learn the skills that interest him the most. Raju learned video editing and animation. He launched his own YouTube channel and uploaded new videos every week. Over time, Raju gets another source of income. Ramu continues to take pleasure in his leisure time.

Tell me, Ramu or Raju, who should be more concerned about the future? Without a doubt, Ramu will be heartbroken the day he is fired from his job. The moral of the story is that if we value our time now, it will pay off in many ways in the future. It will offer you both financial and time freedom in your life.

13th rule: Ramu and Raju both work for the same company. Both of them have excellent time management skills. But Ramu consistently finishes his assignment much ahead of Raju. Why does this happen all the time? While you are working, the only thing that truly matters is your focus. If you can't focus, you will consistently deliver late, regardless of how well you understand and practice time management concepts.

14th rule: Time is energy. Working with the right team saves your energy. If you train your employees properly, you can reduce the amount of time and energy you spend on continuous monitoring and supervision. With the right guidance and motivation, you can teach your employees to do more tasks. If you don't get the right feedback, you'll waste time on things that didn't cause any problems. Good standards will eliminate daily issues that might otherwise consume your time and energy.

Try to say "no" to many things to save energy. When you say no to things that you cannot control or that are not important, you save your time for meaningful yes.

People have a lot of trouble keeping track of their time. They don't know how to use their time well. The reason is there are many things we can't control. The majority of our time is wasted on things we have no control over. Your life will be free of frustration if you focus on activities that you have control over. We waste our emotional, physical, and mental energy on things that are beyond our control.

15th rule: Like the guidelines, deadlines are keys to keeping your time on track. Watching football matches, you may have noticed that players play very aggressively when a team is behind goals. They create 300 percent more opportunities to score a goal than before the opposing team scores. Without a tight estimated timeframe, nobody takes the tasks seriously, and cannot be completed more quickly.

There is no work that can be done tomorrow because there is no guarantee that tomorrow will come for you.

If you don't follow the rules above, you're in trouble. Unfortunately, what we typically do is "shorten our time" available. Daily firefighting, repeating mistakes, working with average talent, unproductive tasks, being full of distractions, and having no standards at work all shorten our time.

Here is an incident that happened a few months ago. A manager from a manufacturing company emailed me. Ranjith: Whatever you said to me regarding time management is agreed upon. But I want to make you aware that it is not working for me. I don't know why.

After the fact check, I replied to him, "Dear Sir, I'm glad you at least tried to implement time management principles. But you might have been wrong about how to manage your time. Time management is important for everyone who works in a company. To get the most out of it, you need to involve everyone. If your priorities are different from those of the others in your organization, it will never work out."

He was setting priorities and organizing his time. But due to many problems at the workplace, he couldn't manage his time as well as he had planned. Most of the time was spent on problem-solving, micromanaging, and supervision.

The time of a manager is different from that of a worker. A manager should be aware of what not to do so that employees will know what to do. Otherwise, you will most likely interfere with all tasks, and your employees will be unable to manage their priorities. If a manager is micromanaging, it is clear that he is not doing his job well and is not letting others do theirs.

At the end of the day, if you are not satisfied with how things went, rethink and restructure your time and list your priorities again.

People often say I have no time for myself, my workflow is heavy, and I am stressed. I can't balance my life. I have one question for you: tell me how many hours you'll work. Ten to twelve hours a day at most. Still, you have more than half the time remaining. You can work on your passion, spend time with family and friends, and you can travel and explore many things. There are many things you can do aside from work. If you spend your time on unwanted things, you will always complain that you have no time.

The problem is not that you are stressed at work; it is that you have nothing to do after work. No passion and no purpose This is how you can transition from a mechanical life to a more meaningful one. Your life is mechanical if you're trapped in a 9–5 job. By the end of the day, you will be bored, tired, and angry. But if you embrace your job like a game and have hobbies outside of it, you may transform your life from a mechanical one to a more meaningful one. Fill your time with greater adventures. You will never complain after that. But it is not affordable for many.

Take some time to relax and hang out with family and friends. Most of the time at work, you're with your co-workers and customers. This doesn't have anything to do with you or your life. You are more than your work. Having a good balance between your personal life and your work life will give you more energy to get through hard times. The best time spent is with the people you care about, not in your office or your boss's cabin.

Spend time discovering a variety of things. God has given us only this moment. When you feel miserable, that moment is gone. You can exchange your bad feelings for good ones. If you are really under stress or work pressure, take a month off and explore the wonders of nature. If you can take frequent breaks to explore your life, you will feel much better when you go back to work.

This is something we can learn from a kid. When a child is playing and breaks a toy, he will cry. But if you give them a new toy, they'll enjoy it just as much as they did before. This is what we must do. We always waste our time crying about the things we leave behind or the things we miss. But we don't know how beautiful it could be until we get out of that situation.

Your life is a reflection of the time you have spent on important things. There isn't much more time for us to spend here. We only have one life. But this one life is made up of many different types: social, family, professional, personal, and spiritual.

The quality of your family life could suffer if you don't make time to spend with them. If you don't spend enough time at work, your career might fail. If you don't get along with people, your social life will struggle. If you don't spend time on yourself, you can't grow, and if you don't spend time on spiritual growth, you'll never find the meaning of your life.

Thinking In Design: World in A New Light

You can only manage, control, and optimize your business with an efficient design, not through a series of meetings!!!

No one can explain specifically why we humans have one heart but two kidneys. If we had an extra heart, we'd have lived much longer. We can still survive if we donate one of our kidneys. The anatomy of our design is both mysterious and stunning. Our lives and the entire universe have been shaped by the natural design process.

I'd like to believe that the Big Bang was the first design process ever known to us. As a consequence of this event, our planet, mother Earth, was created.

The second design process that took place here was the development of our habitat and the evolution of all living things. This was the most exciting step in the design process. What if photosynthesis functioned in the opposite direction, using oxygen to produce carbon dioxide? Could it be possible for us to live here? We are in the second phase of the natural design procedure and heading toward the final phase.

The final and third design process will be the destruction of our lives and our planet. It might be a nuclear war, climate change, an alien attack, drought, or an asteroid strike. We have no idea. But in this design process, we have got more influence than the other two.

The rhinoceros, for example, has existed for more than 55 million years. They endured everything, including meteor strikes, earthquakes, and drought. But in the last few decades, due to human activity, they have all been on the verge of extinction (very few remain), which is quite sad.

However, the duration of the existence of everything in the universe is pivotal. What if dinosaurs never died out? Any kind of life on Earth would have become impossible. The extinction of every species will happen, but we don't know how and when.

Have you ever wondered why one product or service is usually preferred over another? Why do certain businesses consistently perform well and achieve a high rate of return? It is not about how much money they spend or how efficient their system is; it is about the quality of the mind that drives the organization. They have already figured out why, when, what, and how to think smartly in every situation. Each exceptional work is the culmination of an extraordinary intellectual process.

A customer's utilization of your product or service is vital to your success. What is the point if your product or service cannot relate to it on a human level? We don't need to develop anything that is for the use of robots, right?

Have you ever questioned why your once-thriving business is suddenly faltering for no apparent reason? That's because you haven't upgraded your thinking for a very long time. You eventually got stuck in your comfort zone because you were happy with what you had accomplished. Any person who appreciates the status quo above everything is likely to resist any attempts to change their methods.

To solve a problem efficiently, we must dive into the problem. The key component, however, is to think in a certain way to arrive at the most workable solution. If you bring Sherlock Holmes to a crime scene, he will arrive at a different conclusion than any other police officer there. If you can think of the best possible solution to any problem, you'll stand out from the crowd.

If we can think beyond logic and rules, we can find solutions more creatively. For our own convenience and to avoid confusion, we set rules. For instance, my bicycle was stolen from my residence, and I lodged a police complaint. It has been nearly a year since I received a response.

Let's find a solution that defies logic. After missing my bicycle, I went to the police station to file a complaint. What if I could choose a date to get my bicycle back from the thief? If the police do not return my bicycle within a month, the government will be responsible for my loss. I would propose a law mandating that I can choose the time to get my stolen things back because the loss is mine. Otherwise, the thief will continue to steal until he is caught. What if he is never arrested by the police? How many bicycles will he steal in his lifetime? Whose responsibility is this?

Our lives and businesses are structured around a succession of continuous problem-solving situations. Consequently, a good outcome depends more on one's thinking style. You are paid fairly well, not because of how you speak, appear, or act, but because you are capable of handling even the most challenging problems with incredibly simple solutions.

The most challenging task is figuring out how to solve an issue without creating another. Here's a good example: We often hear on the news that a large number of trees must be felled to make way for road or railway construction. But we, as a public, vehemently oppose it. (On the contrary, we cut down trees on our property to build a house or commercial complex).

Then what is the most effective solution for addressing this issue? Roads or rail are the most viable options to increase connectivity from one city to another. Constructing roads or railway tracks is not the problem, but unscientific urban planning, ineffective waste management, overconsumption, and overpopulation are the problems. We are protesting the situation; instead, we should seek a long-term solution.

We need to "think outside the box," a phrase we've often heard. But many of us hop out of the box and sit inside another one. This is why trying to solve problems ends up creating other problems.

To solve any problem and run a happy business, we need to adopt three different types of thinking styles: "thinking in design", "first-principles thinking", and "thinking in systems".

Thinking in Design

There is already a systematic and effective method for executing the design thinking process; it has been accepted for a long time and is generally known. It will help you start from scratch to create something new.

Extraordinary improvement is a result of a new method of organizing work. This sentence inspired me to think about how I could look at the problem in a different way to find better solutions. I began to look at the problem from many different perspectives. But every model I tried had two things in common: the form (the way things are now) and the function (the current activities of the form). Again, I did some experiments and found that the most creative solutions come from rearranging the current form and function and adding the element of perfection.

It is so important to look at the form and function of anything since every company is different. You cannot achieve greatness by copying the practices of a successful company. It will not function that way. The structure and functioning of your processes and systems will differ from those of other companies. This approach will allow you to see the problem as it is and find the best solutions.

The Taj Mahal and Tirupati Temple are some of the most evocative examples of the sophisticated design thinking of ancient times. It is an incredibly unconventional way of thinking. Shah Jahan built a tomb for his wife, expending millions of rupees at a time when nobody else had ever done so. As a result, the whole world may now marvel at the wonderful edifice that defied predictions and evolved into one of the contemporary world's wonders.

According to legend, the construction of the Tirupati temple began 2500 years ago. It stands 853 meters above the ground, which is taller than the Burj Khalifa, which is the world's tallest building right now. Can you challenge this design-thinking process today? Perhaps not!

These are just two examples; our ancient design concepts continue to have an impact on our lives today. For example, look at how astrology works. Do we ever wonder why we can remember everything that has happened in the past but not what will happen in the future? Astrology provided the solution to this conundrum. Even though we have the most advanced technologies, we still need to know how and why the Egyptian pyramids were constructed. This proves our ancestors were masters of the design thinking process.

The point is thinking in design begins when we question and challenge conventional order and behaviour. We must have a better understanding of the process or a system that requires a solution.

You will develop a learner's attitude if you approach problems like a freshman. When you approach something as a learner, you will try to gather as much information as possible. However, you might not understand anything new from a situation if you approach it like you already know it because you will attempt to come up with a solution based on your past experience. That is not how design thinking works. You must always have a learner's attitude.

Thinking in design makes it easier to make changes in the stages of the process where you have more problems.

I'll describe the design thinking process by focusing on its three key points: form, function, and perfection. A form is the current appearance of your process, a function is the tasks assigned to its form, and perfection is the greatest value that can be derived from both form and function.

For example, take two-wheelers for instance. The form is what we all know; the function is to take you from one point to another; and Perfection is contingent upon how well energy efficiency, aesthetics, materials, quality, intelligence, endurance, types, and competitiveness are. Those who get a bigger market share will have products that look good, work well, and are perfect.

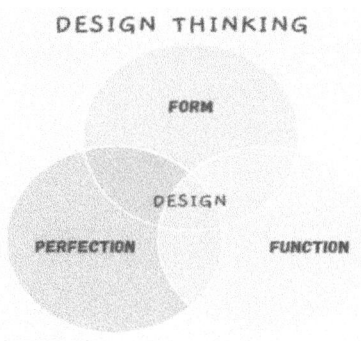

Here, I will describe design thinking from different perspectives so that you can grasp the concept in a better way possible.

Just look at our forests as a form where millions of animals reside. The function of a forest is to feed and protect millions of animals and birds, not the other way around. But we cut down the forest cover every year for industrialization, mining, livestock feeding, and farming. We are ruining the natural environment, which is important for our survival and well-being. People are upset about climate change, the loss of wildlife, and pollution.

If our design isn't "empathetic", it's clear that we won't get good results. This is why our nature frequently malfunctions. We are all responsible for everything that goes wrong in the world. We can't always blame certain people or processes when something goes wrong.

When I was in school, one of my classmates' parents had an accident and needed blood transfusions. We were having fun while the teachers were busy finding a blood donor. We were thinking we'd be free and could play all day. Today, though, I wonder if I would be enjoying the day as much if my parents had been injured. No, not even close. I sincerely regret that moment today. In the world we live in now, what we lack is empathy—empathy toward the poor, animals, elderly people, and nature.

Many notable figures, such as Ratan Tata, Dr Abdul Kalam, and Abraham Lincoln, are well known for their empathy. All the brilliant people who made history had one thing in common: they all had empathy. Moreover, it is the cornerstone of thinking in design.

No person in history achieved success for selfish reasons. Being empathetic is the only way to make a difference in the world.

The design of the Tata Nano car is the perfect example of Mr Ratan Tata's empathetic behaviour. When Ratan Tata decided to make a car like the Nano, it showed that it is possible to make a car for less than one lakh rupees. But why didn't Nano get the expected result?

The design of the car was good, the price was affordable, and the quality was good. We are the ones who look for flaws in everything before appreciating them. Our society is based on people's social standing. We believe that if I buy a Nano car, everyone else will assume that I cannot afford a good car. I think the Nano is the best car ever made, in the history of cars.

Give me one good reason why he would decide to make a car for one lakh rupees, which was virtually impossible. Was it to add a few more million to his savings? No. He intended to help middle-class families in our country afford a car; it may have been a market failure, but it will be remembered forever in the history of automobiles. There are many case studies on how the Tata Nano became a failure, but no one really talks about the story behind the Nano car. It could be the most inspiring story in the history of car design evolution.

Likewise, consider an empathic perspective the next time you want to tackle a process-related issue. It is likely that many new possibilities will arise when you do so.

For example, putting pressure on employees is an easy thing to do when you have a tight schedule. However, if you tackle the situation by reducing Muda and maximizing efficiency, you may achieve a better outcome due to its emotional aspect.

Let me give you another perspective on why it's important to think about design when building our homes. When was the last time you saw a bird building its nest? Look at the form; it is unique, the functions are proper, and the design, material, size, utility, and the amount of effort and time they spent on its construction are all flawless. This is why it is called a "perfect home".

But we live in a home, which is probably a concrete box. We never question the shape of our home. For us, the form of a house is just an appearance. However, the form should be a message, not just a physical look. The form should be both visually and technically challenging. Relying only on past data to develop a form makes the process easy, but challenging the future is difficult.

When we think of home, we envision a place where the family can spend time together. A home is a place where we must consider waste management, comfort, cleanliness, aesthetics, air circulation, energy consumption, and, today, most importantly, a nuclear bunker; it is, after all, a place for well-being and safety.

We all like to dine at well-known restaurants but rarely enjoy eating at home. I feel quite uneasy doing deep work at home. When I am in a temple, I feel quite tranquil, but when I get home, I feel tired. When I'm in a library, I want to read books, but not at home. When we are in our own homes, we have the impression that we are in some sort of cage. There is something fundamentally wrong with our idea of home.

We need powerful design concepts that can challenge the current forms. A form is a creative mind's manifestation. For example, I like pet animals. What if my definition of a home includes not only me but also my pets? I want to live comfortably with my family and my pets. My pets spend their time as though they were in their natural habitat. When creating a form, most of us overlook this empathetic approach.

The function is the maximum utility value of the form. The function is the connection between you and your home. I want my home to elevate my emotions and passions. My home should participate in my growth. When we think of a building as a home, we have no functional ideas. A home is either 2 BHK or 3 BHK. We measure in terms of area, not utility. When we are limited in function, we never achieve perfection. The function is the form's adaptability in all aspects. Then, via interactions with the information we have, a proper function can be established.

Perfection is the state of having precisely accomplished what is desired. Perfection is achieved via careful selection, preparation, execution, feedback, and a lot of trial-and-error methods. Perfection has levels. We can't reach perfection the first time, may it be. It is like making a movie. No one can make a great movie in a single take. It takes several years of preparation, practice, creativity, teamwork, hard work, attention to detail, and innovation (a competitive edge).

When other people find your work admirable, you can confidently label it "perfect". Continuous and conscious practice is required to achieve perfection. Perfection is reached when we do it with complete devotion, dedication, and determination. When we add only value-added functions to the form, we naturally reach perfection. Perfection means deleting many functions that are not suitable for our form.

To reach perfection, you need to have the capacity to know how good is good enough. Our pride and overconfidence lead us to believe that anything we create on our own must be a perfect piece of art. But this is called perceived perfection, not actual perfection. There is a difference between perceived perfection and actual perfection. Reaching a state of perfection is trickier than we think.

In a nutshell, designing a form requires creative ideas, determining its functions requires scientific reasoning, and reaching perfection requires an innovative approach. Building a balance between these three elements (form, function, and perfection) will create a new experience.

For example, we need a design-thinking approach in our healthcare system today. I know a farmer who had ten acres of land. At the age of ten, he began working on the family farm alongside his father. He is currently in his seventies. He's the father of two girls. He ensured a comfortable life for them. Both his daughters are married and settled in a city far from their village. His wife was diagnosed with cancer. To save his wife, he sold his land and burned all his life savings. Unfortunately, she couldn't survive.

Now, he doesn't have a single penny of his savings, despite working hard for the last fifty years. This is not a single case. It is high time to fix our healthcare system; otherwise, the majority of our people will continue to struggle with finance if they have to go to any hospital for treatment.

When we don't question the order, we never change our educational system, health care system, political system, infrastructure, businesses, or our lives. We can't change anything.

Here is an industry example. Let's say you are experiencing difficulties with employee output. What is the form here? Your employees. Consider the form from many different perspectives: what unproductive employees do all day, how they are selected, what their roles are, how to measure their skills, and what are their academic qualifications. Then, analyse the functions. What's missing in functions, exactly, that's holding performance down? Add functions that can solve it, such as training, a clear job description, defining responsibilities, setting goals, etc.. Now is the time to immediately put your ideas into action. You'll eventually improve your employee productivity through a series of trial-and-error strategies.

Next time when you face a problem at work, try using this design philosophy by thinking about it in terms of form and function. You can easily come up with better options.

The below-shown image is one of our ancient temple architectures. Can you make this stone carving more beautiful? I bet you can't because it reaches the state of real perfection.

Thinking In Systems: We Are Interdependent

Everything in this universe is connected in complex ways and works as a single, perfect system. Our business is a subsystem of our economy. Our economy is a subsystem of our people. Our people are a subsystem of nature. Our planet is a subsystem within the solar system. We cannot avoid or escape this web of reality.

Assume that your business depends heavily on one or two key people. Explain how they will run the business. It's obvious that they'll run it the way they would like. If they aren't smart, that will affect your business. But how will they run a business if a company keeps a set of high-yield systems that can be measured? Yes, of course. If the system is followed, everyone is valued equally, and the desired result will be achieved.

Moscow University has recently published a research paper on future jobs titled "Atlas of Emerging Jobs." It is developed by over 2500 specialists with collaboration from leading multinational corporations. According to their study, 57 present-day occupations would become obsolete by 2030, while 186 new occupations would arise. They claimed in their in-depth study report that, to run a successful company, you must excel in a few key traits, and one of them is systems thinking.

A century ago, there was a company that manufactured cars. The person who owned the car company was brilliant. He wanted to reduce the price of the cars and increase the factory's output. He wanted everyone to be able to afford to buy a car, which can only be possible if the prices are low. Back then, the idea of mass production wasn't established. He was smart enough to understand the fact that telling workers to speed up the process would only work if managers were on the shop floor with them, which is very impractical.

He was not thinking of increasing the headcount or expanding the manufacturing facilities, which was the only solution back then. His idea was to increase productivity with the help of something novel. His concept was to accelerate the process so that he could sell more cars at a lower price to everyone in the world. He went to a slaughterhouse once, where he saw all the animals lined up on a moving conveyor belt to make it easier for the workers to do their jobs quickly and efficiently. He was evaluating the possibilities of adopting this system in his car production unit.

To figure out how to turn this idea into reality, he did some research and consulted with scientists and industrial experts. Three more years passed before the assembly line concept was introduced in his factory. The rest was history.

What if he continued to use conventional manufacturing methods that rely heavily on employees' skill levels? He believed in the system instead. It shows the world that workers with or without experience can easily work together to achieve a common goal with the help of a system.

He revolutionized the manufacturing industry. The time required to produce a single car was reduced from twelve hours to ninety-three minutes. The profit margin skyrocketed. The price of a car was reduced from $850 to $260. Time, money, and resources are employed to prepare for the future.

This concept was later dubbed the "assembly line" since it was a speedy production method. It was Mr Henry Ford who made this concept possible. He instituted a significant shift away from handmade craftsmanship and toward assembly line production. Assembly lines revolutionized production in the modern era, not just for automobile manufacturers, but also for manufacturers of mobile phones, food, toys, beverages, and a variety of other sectors.

When mass production began, there was another big issue. A car contains more than ten thousand parts. It is not economically feasible to manufacture all of those parts in a single company. A technical fault in one part can potentially wreck the whole vehicle. However, one company has taken this matter very seriously. The company noticed that people get easily bored when they do the same job over and over again, so there was a lot of job turnover. Due to the stringent rules of the assembly line method that had to be followed, the employees received no rewards. There wasn't a proper method to address the issue right away, so the finished vehicle required rework. Numerous vehicles have been called after major failures. This is because they failed to identify the problems on the spot.

Every system is dynamic in nature. It requires maintenance and marginal improvements, or it will not be as efficient as it was on the first day.

One company devised an innovative approach to address this problem. The most effective method for speeding up the process and lowering the failure rate is identifying and removing the waste at the source. During the research, they found seven wastes in a manufacturing setup. They developed a system that accurately measures the variations in a process. This systematic approach is widely known as the "Toyota Production System." Once again, this method transformed the whole automobile industry.

Throughout their research, they realized that the effectiveness of the system approach depends on the active participation of every employee. To operate the system effectively, you must adopt a people-centric approach. As a result, they began rewarding their employees. They started giving promotions to employees who made a significant contribution. The Kaizen philosophy was brought in to improve the efficiency of all operations.

Whenever you want to improve the efficiency of your business, "thinking in systems" will help you. Gather as much data as possible about the issue from as many sources as possible. Figure out the nature of all those data; look for connections between the data. You will find the answer. It is difficult and risky, and may lead to a lot of confusion. But still, it is one of the best ways to eliminate all your bottlenecks because everything is connected, structurally and meaningfully. Every solution lies hidden in the system if we can connect the dots.

McDonald's and Asian paintings are some of the best examples of the extraordinary success of system thinking. McDonald's is well-known for both its hamburgers and its service. People acknowledge the system for its dependability and quality of food. Their suppliers and franchisees have been instructed to work with McDonald's, not work for McDonald's. In this system approach, the McDonald's burger tastes the same as it does anywhere else in the world.

In the 1950s, the Asian Paints plant in Maharashtra employed 1,600 workers, whereas in the 1980s, the Ankleshwar plant in Gujarat, which had the same capacity, employed only 250 workers. They optimized their processes with the help of a system and adopted automation technology. Automation cannot be implemented in a process without optimization. Only a successful system is capable of performing optimization.

Understanding our interdependence provides a useful framework for characterizing teamwork. In other words, it's the realization that a well-knit group is crucial to success. A housekeeping guy is as important as a manager in an organization. The concept is precise and definitive.

We tend to think that if something works well for other businesses, it should work well for us too. Success is the compound effect of the value you create over time. Success is the ability to convert input into deliverables in the most profitable way. For that, many things should come together and work with great balance. When you see the greatness of others, that is the surface-level story of success.

Asian paints, for instance, are known for their well-organized supply chains. It's the single most important reason for their accomplishments. But if you try to copy their model, it will not work for you. Because they have been analysing supply chain data for over 75 years, and if you try to replicate that model, it does not work. You cannot undermine their trust by imitating their model. But if you think in terms of design, you can figure out how to break that link.

All organizations are part of an open system, which means interaction with the outside world. The degree of interaction may vary. Those who can develop a strong connection with the system will benefit the most. For example, Apple Inc. is a subsystem of the huge consumer electronics market. One of their products is the iPhone.

The iPhone's manufacturing strategy is one of the best examples of today's global manufacturing ecosystem. The iPhone is designed in the US, with major supply chains from China, Europe, the US, and Asia. The iPhone is primarily manufactured and assembled in China by a Taiwanese company, and sold all across the world. This is how Apple maintains high profits and low manufacturing costs with the help of systems thinking.

If the iPhone were manufactured in the United States, the company's operational expenses might increase by more than $5 billion. It would also take many years to scale up production, including developing the infrastructure, crafting the skill sets, and training the workforce.

Systems thinking is a highly structured and standardized way of doing things. With the help of a system, we can measure, analyse, control, and improve every event in a business, which is crucial for manufacturing excellence.

This is the reason why you can't run your company with the people you like, you can't run your company for selfish motives, you can't run your company to grow yourself, you can't run a company without a plan, you can't run a company without a vision, you can't do every job in your company, you can't ignore the changes, and you can't underestimate the importance of unity.

For example, to increase the profit margin, you imagine lowering the salaries would be a good idea. What will happen now? Nobody except your lowest-performing employees will want to stick around because neither you nor your company is important to them. They quit whenever they want. They will create countless problems each day. All this doesn't bother you, though, because your attention is somewhere else.

One day, however, you will have to awaken from your fantasy world and confront the real world. By that time, your quality has gone down, your customers have gone, your reputation is gone, your investment is gone, and everything you have earned over time is gone. A profit-seeking mindset leads to bankruptcy. The efficacy of systems thinking can be seen in action here.

Many school dropouts achieved the highest success than anyone else in history, which doesn't mean that if you drop out of school, you can accomplish a lot of things in life. If we could figure out the perfect formula for performance that could apply to anyone, then the Chinese country would already have tonnes of the highest-performing athletes. However, still it couldn't because performance depends on the abilities of each person, and there are unknown factors that ultimately decide the outcome.

Linear relationships are simple to understand. If you need twice more rotis than yesterday, you need twice the amount of atta. But this is not the case for everything. You do not need twice as many employees if you are doubling your output.

As parents, we push our kids to study hard so they can be like someone who did well in school and went on to be successful. This is because our thinking is linear. This is the reason our lives are extremely stressful. Life is about finding the right balance. Even if you have a degree from Harvard or Stanford, you will be fired if you can't do your job well than others.

Every action has consequences, and every consequence has repercussions of its own. Small changes in a complex system led to sudden and significant changes. When we change some aspects of a complex system, we always bring about effects that we didn't plan for. If we can think of a second-order effect, we choose our actions more carefully. We usually think at the first level when we plan for changes. But we can make good decisions if we can think beyond the first level and ask ourselves many times, "What will happen secondary if we make this choice now?"

Thinking In First Principle: From the Source

In one of his writings, Bhagat Singh outlined the traits of revolutionary thinking as merciless criticism and independent thinking. I completely agree with him. In today's society, neither of these characteristics exists.

No one knows where the idea of "first principle thinking" has come from, but there are quotes from Aristotle that indicates he used to try this method to solve problems that were hard to find a better solution. He quoted, "the first point from which we know something."

Today, Mr Elon Musk promotes this idea everywhere he works. When he was asked about his preferred method of problem-solving, he stated that "thinking from first principles" allowed him to uncover the most efficient answers to real-world problems. In the highly industrialized world of today, it enables us to devise the most cost-effective solutions. It also encourages us to think independently.

It is assumed that the first principle of thinking cannot be deduced further. Is it simple to do? First-principal thinking is difficult to teach, so let's learn from some real-world examples. Let's analyse the major inflection points in Elon Musk's life that stemmed from his ability to think in terms of the first principle.

When Elon was young, he was afraid of the dark. He didn't want to spend the night alone. When he realized that darkness was just a result of a lack of photons, he no longer feared the darkness. He always desired to think like a scientist. Scientists never presume anything. They ask questions to get to the core of the matter. They don't use comparisons. When you observe and think a little deeper, you will have the advantage.

After founding PayPal, he wished to launch a rocket manufacturing company. To learn more about rockets, he travelled to Russia to purchase cheaper rockets. He realized that purchasing a rocket is prohibitively expensive, as it may cost over $70 million. He returned to the United States and pondered how to make rockets more affordable.

Using the "first principal method," he began to estimate the components of a rocket, such as aluminium, copper, titanium, metals, and alloys, which were suitable for use in space. He then tried to figure out how much it was worth on the commodity market. He realized that the cost of a rocket's materials represented only 2% of the total price. He saw this as an opportunity to save money. He subsequently established the Space Exploration Company and recruited renowned rocket engineers and technical teams to assist in the design of the rockets. Within a few years, he had roughly tenfold reduced the cost of rocket manufacturing.

An even more interesting fact is fact that he never got a formal education in rocket science. He did that because he was capable of thinking in the first principle. In the future, he might set up a factory where rockets can be manufactured in an assembly line.

Take another example: His Tesla car company is one of the most innovative and successful car brands in the world. He branded his car as not just a vehicle but technology on wheels. When he was attempting to design and develop a cost-effective battery pack for his tesla car, he employed the first principle thinking once again.

The battery pack is the most significant component of an electric vehicle. It costs $600 to produce one kWh, which is not affordable to the general population. He began to think in terms of first principles. He broke down the components that make the battery packs, and they altogether cost only $70 to $80 or 10% of the real cost. He then devised the most cost-effective way to mass-produce the battery packs.

This is how Elon Musk used to think and figure out how to find a solution to every important problem. But it is more difficult than we think. For example, a rocket has many parts, and the technology is sensitive and high-tech. If a system doesn't work, we can't take a screwdriver and fly into the sky to fix it. Building a system is not that easy. It takes a lot of hard work, trying things out, and fixing problems over and over again. Research and development require significant time and resources. It takes courage, involvement, and a strong will. Most importantly, the ability to think independently.

When we first look at any problem, it seems simple, and we assume that it does not need any intervention as we look at the problems at their surface level. In a company, two supervisors always argued on the shop floor. Each despised the other. But it didn't bother the manager at all. He believed conflict in the workplace is normal and necessary. But later, their fight became more serious, and one of the supervisors stabbed the other with a knife. It was easy to think that the argument was normal, but the hidden side of the hatred became bloodshed. When we examine things casually, we feel that we don't need a novel solution.

I conducted an experiment to determine why employees are more miserable at work. When I asked the managers for ideas, they all said one thing in common; our workers don't care about what they do. They are only here to take payment. They are unwilling to follow our instructions. One thing I want to clarify here is that we never try to make others follow our instructions. Humans are not built for that. However, using first-principle thinking, I come to a very fundamental conclusion.

Four aspects influence the satisfaction of a worker in a company;

They believe that they are underachievers.

They have no career-related expectations or any future plans.

They consider themselves bad communicators, regardless of whether they express their feelings, give their opinions and suggestions, or communicate their ideas.

They worry that nobody is helping them at work.

These were the cause, and if we can resolve them, we can create a much happier workplace. When employees are happy in their jobs, they consistently produce excellent results. However, if we assume they are not committed to the company and their jobs, we will always push them to follow the instructions. That won't lead to anything meaningful.

The "5 Why" analysis can also be linked to the first principle of thinking. It is similar but not the same. Once a manager had to do a "5 why" analysis to find a solution, but even after the analysis, he couldn't come up with a solution. I told him to go with three or four extra whys, such as a 7-Why or 8-Why analysis. He made fun of me. He told me we couldn't go beyond "5 why". Because he was considering it a standard form, not thinking of its function.

Let me use the context of manufacturing battery packs for electric cars to show some of the common ways of thinking in the workplace. These are the superficial thinkers in the workplace.

Assumption-based thinking: In this way of thinking, one might believe that the battery pack of an electric vehicle is the critical component and would be impractically expensive to manufacture. It is extremely difficult to source raw materials because the supply chain is not well established. Due to the high cost of production, most people cannot afford it. It would be a waste of resources even to try. These are superficial thinkers. People who hold this view always emphasize the advantages of the outcomes. These types are predominantly selective listeners.

These people always work under stress because they have poor communication skills. They miss out on opportunities because they rarely ask why.

They are always judgmental because they fear the change. There are more chances that our initial judgment could be wrong.

Experience-based thinking: In this mode of thinking, one would always act as if they are more knowledgeable than everyone else. They will conclude that this would not work because a combustion engine is too convenient, and consumers would not choose an electric engine over a diesel engine. Most people wouldn't even think about buying an electric car because of global warming and pollution. They will compare the sales data of combustion engines vs electric vehicles over the years. They will demonstrate how lengthy the recharging process is, and today time is the most luxurious commodity. Setting up a production unit for a battery pack is going to be very expensive. They can't imagine anything outside of the box. Their experience is their box.

A consultant was hired at the factory where I worked some time ago. His job was to improve our company's systems and standards better. On the new project, management chose me to collaborate with him. I spent close to fifteen minutes with him on our first day together. We had a casual conversation on the first day. He told my management that my knowledge was too limited. That is the problem with this type of thinker. They judge too quickly, and their only reference point is their experience. They will say I have thirty years of experience, which means his core experience is repeated over thirty years. That's it. These people always want to impress others.

It might work somewhere, but it might not work everywhere.

Model-based thinking: In his type of thinking, someone would develop a model to predict the outcome. Make a roadmap of what it looks like if it is a success or a failure. They will look at the other electric car companies and use their balance sheet to predict the future. It can only help to design a model from past events. These models only help to organize information. But it will never help to think about something new. They use old case studies and other inferences to come up with a solution.

Every model, practice, and experience is ineffective, but some will work. But nothing works better than first-principle thinking.

Guidance: Standing At The Front

Some managers are chasing people, and some are chasing a dream. Those who have no dreams will naturally chase people. Today, a company requires people-skilled managers rather than people-focused managers.

During my interviews with managers, I often ask them where they see themselves and their company in ten years. Most of the responses I received were like this: "Profit margin is too low to invest in; I don't know how to survive", "market is too competitive now", "the future is unknown to everyone", and so on. How can a manager lead a company if they don't know what's going to happen in their company? How can they plan for the future if they believe that everything is short-term and uncertain? If the future is unpredictable, what are you doing today?

Leadership is an innate quality that emanates from within. It isn't anything that can be taught or learned. It is like kindness: no one can teach you how to be kind; it comes naturally. Likewise, leadership is a natural trait;

one cannot become a good leader unless he or she is made for it. It is the reality.

Leadership is necessary for all organizations, regardless of the company's size. If you are not responsible for bringing your company to the next level, then working as a manager will not benefit you or your company. Those in charge of small organizations often fail to see the need for strong leadership.

A person who is in charge of a company must meet "nine key responsibilities," which are,

"Functioning at optimum capacity"

"Maximum control over costs"

"Attract talent and build synergy"

"Profit year after year"

"Customer focus"

"Conflict management"

"Set and accomplish long-term goals"

"Implement changes quickly"

"Set a suitable working condition"

Nobody in the organization will be more concerned with these nine responsibilities than the leader. These are the jobs that every leader has to be aware of. The rest of the qualities, like empathy, insight, humility, optimism, innovation, empowerment, honesty, proactiveness, creativity, and integrity, are not everyone's cup of tea. You can always be a responsible leader, but not a successful one.

You do not need to emulate the lifestyles of other famous leaders in the world. Even if you try, you'll never become one of them. If you can't handle all the above-listed duties, you can't call yourself a responsible leader. But you don't need to consider anything if your motive is just to survive.

In a company, guidance is a force that comes from the objective of doing business. Only a vision can guide an organization to its full potential. To have a vision, you need to have a strong desire and intention. No one can guide a company in the right direction without good intentions.

Tata Indica was the first passenger car designed and manufactured entirely in India, and every Indian should be proud of it. What led Ratan Tata to make Indica the first car made in India? When Ratan Tata envisioned a fully Indian-made car, everyone told him it couldn't be done without a partnership with an international car company. But he believed that India could manufacture its own car.

If you have a strong desire and good intentions, even if you face many reasons to give up, you don't quit. After many setbacks and hard times, Ratan Tata finally made it possible. The Tata Indica was the first car successfully made in India and captured 20% of the market share in a very short period.

Building trust is an essential leadership responsibility. Everything begins to grow once trust is established. Trust strengthens the connection between you and everyone else involved in the process. People will have greater faith in you if you have an open mind. People will listen to you if they can trust you. You can win over your employees if you listen to them more frequently, but not in a meeting-like setting.

Try to keep all the promises you've made to show you are a credible person. Show your employees that you are the most reliable person in the company. Always practice meritocracy in the workplace; when you do so, your employees begin to have greater faith in you. Bring more clarity to whatever you do. Be honest with everything you do. Empower your team while working alongside them. This is how you may earn the confidence of other people.

As a leader, you should always look at the positive side of everything. You should never ask yourself, "Why am I working with this company?" Instead, you should ask, "Does my contribution make this company more productive and profitable?" When the perspective changes, everything changes for the better. You will have more clarity when you start exploring different perspectives.

If you are a manager, build competency in administrative and people skills and do not just focus on technical skills. You will get many people to solve your technical issues, but you need someone to help you with administrative issues. Many managers think solving technical issues is more important and spend 99% of their time on them. But in reality, it is very easy to solve technical issues.

According to my research, the majority of Gen X managers fall into two types: **action-oriented or result-oriented.**

"Go and work", "Don't sit and relax", "Are you here to time pass?" and "your work is too slow" are common phrases from an action-oriented manager.

Most action-oriented managers have worked so hard in the past to get where they are now. So, they have a strong belief that the only way to get results is to work hard. But they forgot the fact that today is the time for smart work, great ideas, and expertise.

An action-oriented manager is perpetually unhappy until everyone follows his exact instructions. They keep track of everyone who disagrees with them and seek ways to fire them later.

Action-oriented managers usually work more than anyone else in the company, like everyday meetings, dealing with problems, micromanaging, and eventually losing control and respect. They don't trust anyone, so the employees don't trust them either.

They like people who work for them day and night but not those who think about a better way to function. They are slightly less in favour of improvement activities because they think that daily tasks, not any improvements, lead to progress. They don't believe much in the trial-and-error method.

They will be happy if people on the shop floor work quickly and run all over the place. They like to see everyone working hard in a factory and push everyone to do the same thing, not because they want to see everyone be productive. There is a big difference between being busy and getting things done.

Action-oriented managers develop short-term stability in a process. The one problem usually seen with this type of manager is that they try to control all the processes instead of just owning them. Most action-oriented managers are short-term thinkers.

They only hire mediocre talents because they don't think it's a big deal just to keep an eye on the process. Focus on action creates a busy workplace, not a productive one.

These types of managers believe that their decisions and methods are perfect for the company's success. So, they try to push workers to follow the instructions. We have always been averse to any kind of input from the employees. Finally, we call it unfair because we work hard, and the results may not appear as favourable.

A Result-oriented Manager: This type of manager would always look for results. "I told you yesterday to finish this today. Why don't you finish it?", "You are fired." That's it. Only the result matters.

Were there any obstacles to completing the job? Could that person better handle the job? Does the team collaborate effectively? Do we need any new technology to improve the results? They won't consider any of those things and don't want to hear anything properly, though.

If you tell them, "Sir, I was having trouble getting the job done," they will respond, "I don't want to hear anything. Complete what I told you." Just one word:

"Finish the work anyhow." They will frequently tell you why I hired you or if you need help from others.

They will never give room for excuses and inconveniences. They may regard improvement efforts as time-wasting activities. We are getting results the way we are working now. There is no need to explore many things; it is a waste of time. They are the most comfortable managers and don't take risks as much as required. They easily get annoyed and refrain from listening to any ideas from anyone.

Under this type of leadership, employees are hesitant to try something new out of fear of being fired. Employees hesitate to ask for help or support from this type of manager. They are afraid of the questions that are going to be asked. "Did you finish it or not?"

They will judge very quickly; they don't ask for reasons. They are non-strategic and give solutions spontaneously without analysing the problem well.

They always focus on lag measures. The best way to do it is by continuously changing people. These types of managers won't be happy with inexperienced and smart employees. The pressure from result-oriented managers is intense for new hires.

They are more transactional. I will give you an offer only if you produce the result. I don't need to listen to the excuses; this is their mantra for work.

This type of manager will look up graphs and charts to feel happy. They are stuck in the same processes that were once successful. They push everyone to follow the same routine, which helps them get results. Even after many years, they resist change because they are afraid of what will happen, if it doesn't work.

But I miss a manager who is '**Process oriented**'. A very low percentage of Gen X managers are process-oriented.

For that matter, we need the perfect mix of action-oriented, result-oriented, and process-oriented managers to guide a company well. When it becomes a combination of these three, we can see a **"transformational manager"**.

If your guidance is incapable of helping people get the work done, then you have a situational risk. It is mainly because all systems are working against you. It is because you are interfering with every process. You need to face a lot of bad situations each day. Situational risk can be reduced by developing teamwork and using technology to track and improve daily work management. Situational risk can be minimized when employees become owners of their work.

Situational risk leads to existential risk, where the company can't help its customers, cannot control the costs, compromises product quality and delivery, and refuses to change. To guide a company, understand the above two situations and find a proper method to analyse all the risks involved and eliminate them one by one.

The greater a person's responsibility, the more likely they are to make a mistake with serious consequences. If an ordinary employee makes a mistake, it can be corrected in five minutes, but if a manager makes a mistake, it may take fifty years to rectify. When we are promoted to managers and supervisors, we believe we have absolute authority and are intelligent enough to never make any mistakes.

This is why Netflix has embraced a standard called "radical Condor", which means anyone can question the management or the CEO about the decisions. If anyone is disinterested in the content they are working on, they can quit their job. Netflix is famous for its radical transparency. Clarity provides confidence and the willpower to make the right decisions.

If you are planning to change the housekeeping method, please ask the janitors how we can do much better because they have much better ideas than you. Most of the risks exist because of poor decisions. The Royal Bank of Scotland failed in 2008. It was shocking news then. The bank committee set up an inquiry to find out what had happened. The cause of the failure was multiple poor decisions made by the CEO of the bank. Unbelievably, nobody questioned any of those foolish decisions.

Culture is the right thing to do the job the right way. Humans and culture are inextricably linked. Culture is what we think, believe, and feel. As per the research, businesses with a good organizational culture tend to be more successful. A good product gives a good experience; likewise, a good company gives a good experience. When you think more inclusively, you can add a lot of value to your workforce.

Today, common sense is rare. A senior business executive I know was working in Mumbai for a multinational company. He used to go to his office by taxi. In Mumbai, the taxi industry halted for two days while the drivers went on strike. For two days, he didn't go to the office because of this reason. Where is common sense? He could have taken the bus, train, or autorickshaw or even asked his colleagues to come and pick him up.

I recently read the news that an employee who came late by twenty minutes was sacked by the company. Their colleagues shared this event in a tweet, saying that he had been working there for the past seven years and had never came late, and this was the first time he came late. Where is common sense?

When Apple dropped many of its products after Steve Jobs's return to the office, this was just a common-sense approach. It was not rocket science to focus on a few things to improve quality and profit.

It was a plain common-sense approach when Unilever reduced its product line from 1,600 to 400 in order to increase margins and accelerate growth.

A leader must have hands-on experience in the process to guide a company well. A manufacturing company in Mumbai appointed a new manager, a highly qualified business manager. He was very strict, highly educated, and hardworking. He wanted to introduce a new culture, new targets, and new goals to achieve, as he did in his previous company. But things got worse as time went on. Daily problems on the shop floor, delivery delays, quality issues, and increased costs of rework and maintenance were very few of them.

When a new manager suddenly wants to change everything, it makes it a bit uncomfortable for employees, and they all resist it. Secondly, he doesn't have any hands-on experience with that particular product and that process. He could have spent time understanding the workers, systems, products, and processes, as well as the organization's history. He could have aligned himself with the existing process and solved one thing at a time. But he wanted to make a radical change and eventually failed to achieve that.

For example, there are X, Y, and Z problems in a company. If a manager does not understand the nature of the problems, how can he resolve them? What if problem X was created by the workers themselves? He struggled very much there, and later, he resigned from the job.

A leader must have the ability to solve problems at both an individual and a company level. Conflicts are part of any business. If you can handle it well without hurting anyone, that's the best way to solve it. It is not enough to be good at customer service; you also need to be able to help out your co-workers when they're having issues.

A company is not made up of a bunch of machines but rather a group of people who are ready to work and spend a major portion of their lives. When everyone is smart and works towards the same objective, the team gets stronger. You will lose control of every process if you fail to guide your workers. In an organization, there is no room for hate, selfishness, or disrespect. I've seen a lot of owners care only about their managers. I have a simple question for you; if you know how to care for your manager, why don't you care about the other people who work for you? Why don't you want to hear any of them?

There is a gap in your business if your current state is far from where you want to be. Most of the time, doing a gap analysis is hard because we often practice the "push approach." We push our employees to do a certain job that they are not capable of handling. Almost every small-scale industry uses this method to fill the gap, but it doesn't work.

Imagine you are the teacher in a jungle. A fish is one of your students. If you try to teach that fish to climb a tree, it will never progress. You will always be disappointed by the results. You will continually consider where the gap is, so you can fill those gaps to teach a fish more efficiently.

When we consider pushing our employees, this is the result. Even if you force someone who lacks the capacity to perform the job, it will not be achieved.

When we all work together, the weakest links cause many problems. The gap gets more prominent when there are more weak spots. And we wanted to push employees to fill the gap that exists. The "push" approach is very common in small businesses and is ineffective in producing results.

Gap assessment works well when we adopt linear thinking. For example, when your machine operator is not good enough for you, it is better to replace the operator rather than appoint a supervisor to guide them.

When you appoint a supervisor to guide the operator, you waste money on both supervisor and the operator. I have seen a lot of companies following this strategy.

Small businesses make a big mistake when they don't quantify their business. Anything that you can measure can be made better. Ask yourself why you are having trouble. If you don't get an answer, you might not have a business model that can be measured. You are just in charge of a regular job.

Respect all individuals and their ideas. Give your employees a space where they can feel their freedom. In times of difficulty, conduct a brainstorming session with your employees. Surprisingly, most of your employees are quite familiar with the issue and may come up with workable solutions. The challenge, however, is with leaders who fail to recognize them.

Many managers continue to believe that asking their employees for ideas and feedback will weaken their authority. This behaviour in the workplace will create a huge intellectual gap between workers and managers. If you don't listen to your employees, they don't want to collaborate. They will do what everyone else is doing and what you tell them to do.

This title is based on the notion that we no longer require leaders but rather guides. Today, almost all information can be found online, and people are less interested in being with a leader and more interested in being with an expert. Only an expert with people skills can lead a whole team. You are a guide only if you can show others that this is the best way to do the job. It is important to be more than just a leader, especially when you have a big impact on many people's lives.

Incompetent leadership is linked with poor financial performance. They either focus excessively on competition or disregard internal conflict. They failed to convince the team to collaborate. It is difficult to achieve financial stability without a motivated workforce.

If you want to lead and guide, you must view learning as a never-ending process. We can learn the most from the little things around us to guide others. Jim Rohn is a well-known American businessman and author. He came up with the term "ant philosophy." We can learn a lot about life and business from an ant. Ants never give up. If they are headed somewhere, you can't stop them. They will always find a way to get there, as if they have no other choice. They are so generous and work well together. Ants have two stomachs, one for themselves and one for sharing food with other ants. Ants are always thinking about the future, which is why they store enough food to last the whole winter.

Guidance is the ability to educate your team in detail about the objectives you desire to achieve, whether they are small or big. It would help if you always valued others' ideas. You should always consider whether your idea is better than others. Attitude is an older version. Rectitude is the new norm. Rectitude is a purposeful mindset that a guide must have.

What you can control, you should. Do not worry about anything that is not in your control. In our lives, we spend most of our time worrying about things that are not in our control.

You cannot control the people; you can only guide them.

You cannot control the outcomes, but you can always work to improve them.

You cannot avoid the situations; you can only manage them.

You cannot control the market; you can only adapt to it. As Bruce Lee said, "Be the water, my dear friends."

We often think the person who can change the company is the only one who works hard. We will start giving more credit to people who seem to work hard. But you never know how much hard work, how many hard workers, or how much favour for hard workers is enough. If you don't know these three things, hardworking employees will always fool you for their benefit.

We believe we could have done a better job predicting how things would turn out. We look at what has worked in the past and assume that's right. We believe these stories, and they form our beliefs. This belief makes it hard for us to make good decisions in the future. We cannot precisely calculate our future, but we can think of it as a probability. We need to let go of many of our ideas, convictions, and past experiences to move forward.

We must be aware that all theories are just educated guesses. When we first learned about the atom, we thought it was the smallest thing on Earth. We thoroughly examined the atoms and learned that atoms are made up of protons, neutrons, and electrons. Then we believed that this was the smallest thing on Earth. Now we know that these particles are made up of smaller particles called quarks, and quarks are made up of smaller particles called hadrons. And we still don't know how many more times we can divide these particles.

All models are wrong, but some can be helpful in the short term. We can only make models based on what has happened in the past. These models may not work in the same way in the future unless we make relative changes to them.

Ask yourself what kind of leader you are. How many qualities do you believe a leader must possess? If you do not find any answers, refer to this title's introduction.

Have you ever thought about why you wanted to do what you are doing now? Asking "why" can help you see the big picture and can help you find the objective of your business.

You may have started your business small, but it is your obligation to grow it to be big, bigger, and biggest.

Positive Psychology: Art of Living

Dr APJ Abdul Kalam delivered a famous speech during the European Union's Golden Jubilee celebrations. He quoted an ancient Tamil poet who stated, "When there is righteousness in the heart, there is beauty in the character, and where there is beauty in the character, there is harmony in the home, and where there is harmony in the home, there is order in the nation. When there is order in the nation, there is peace in the world." This is the fundamental principle of positive psychology.

In the past, psychology has been focused on our weaknesses and emotions and has not given any importance to our strengths and virtues. Positive psychology is a new perspective within psychology that was developed in 1998. The purpose is to understand and promote individual happiness and well-being. It is the scientific study of understanding the happiness, strength, and good qualities in people.

Psychology is an ignored topic in small businesses. Many of us still perceive it as soft science and have no true sense of it. But today, all the branches of psychology are scientifically tested and proven.

Are you aware that two kinds of qualities determine how meaningful our lives will be? Those who "give" and those who "take". What does it mean for someone to be a "Giver"? Giving does not mean that you have to give away everything you own and live like a monk for the rest of your life.

Let me tell you a real-life story to help you understand it better. Someone I know is a good artist. Painting contracts were his main source of income. One time, he looked miserable, so I asked him,

"Hey, what happened? You seem to be very sad."

Then, he told me that he was struggling financially. The painting work no longer helped him earn a living. Unfortunately, he didn't pay his son's school fees. He said, "I can't buy my wife a nice dress; I won't be able to take my family on vacation. I'm extremely sad. I have no idea what to do."

I advised him to take a drawing tuition class for kids so that he could make some money that way.

He smiled and said, "I can't."

"Why?" I asked him, "You are a good artist. It is easy for you to get students."

"Look, I've been getting fewer orders in the last few years, than I used to. There is tough competition. What if someone I teach becomes a talented artist, perhaps even better than me? People would go to them for painting work. Apparently, in the present day, people are looking for digital paintings, about which I know nothing. I am afraid," he honestly explained. I was surprised by his answer. Even after many years, his condition hasn't changed a bit, and he still has a lot of problems. He exemplifies the "taker mindset". His perspective is that of a taker without knowing the opposite, which is the mindset of a giver.

There was another person in our city who was also a painter. When things got hard, he started a coaching centre. He now has two sources of income, one from the painting jobs and the other from his tuition classes.

After that, his life took a remarkable turn. At the same time, he began learning and practicing digital painting. By teaching diverse kids, he learned a lot of things he hadn't paid attention to. He got better at both painting and teaching. As a result of his excellent teaching and good behaviour, he consistently gained new students. He eventually became the best art teacher in our area. He started receiving queries even from outside of our city. He always made positive, strong connections with everyone he met. He opened a small office and built a good small business. He is now the happy owner of a small business.

Who was wrong here? Both were correct in their perspectives. The latter, on the other hand, has a giver mindset, whereas the former has a taker mindset. The benefits of a giver are far superior to those of a taker. Givers are more accomplished individuals than takers because takers are profit-oriented and have a narrow mindset, whereas givers are selfless and pursue happiness and quality of life.

Life is the product of transactions between our inner selves and the external world. The more you give, the more value you create; the more value you create, the more benefits you'll receive. This is how real-world transactions work, right?

How to recognize a giver, people who are always very kind to all and ready to sacrifice for their goals; they are all time happy people who collaborate well with everyone.

In your company, you should have a clear understanding of what to give and what to take. Otherwise, you will always act as a taker, which will inevitably result in failure. Running a business with a taker mindset will severely limit your company's potential.

A positive, open-minded person will lead a much better life than a negative, narrow-minded person. A narrow-minded person will spend their entire life inside a cage. Have you heard a story of a frog in a well? A frog was living at the bottom of a well. He lived his entire life inside the well. One day another frog living in the sea accidentally fell into that well.

Where are you from, the frog asked.

I am from the sea, the other frog replied.

He asked, out of curiosity, whether the ocean is bigger than this well.

The other frog smiled and replied, the size of the sea cannot possibly be compared.

Then, please tell me how big your sea is.

You can't even measure the sea, the other frog answered.

The frog living in the well said you are lying; there is nothing here as larger than my well.

This is the problem with narrow-minded people; they shut off their intellectual and emotional sensibilities.

This era is for people who are passionate and have a positive mindset. You need to be mentally strong to live the way you want to live. There will be times in life when you must face your fate alone, people will avoid you for no apparent reason, and you will be hurt again and again.

When the future is uncertain, take small steps toward your goal, but don't give up on your goal. You should never ask for help to live your own life. When you ask for help, you become a dependent individual right away. Freedom in life lies in standing on our own feet.

Real life begins when we stop comparing ourselves to others. If we always compare ourselves to other people, we will never be happy with what we have. We compare because everything we have is something we've already experienced. We compare because the success of others has always fascinated us. We then try to be successful like them by copying what they do.

One thing we must remember is that imitation is futile. However, if you are trying to imitate others, you should emulate the success criteria they have set for themselves in order to achieve success.

Take, for instance, the life of Mahatma Gandhi; if you wish to copy him, you should not imitate him but rather adopt his guiding principles, such as ahimsa, truth, and morality, as Nelson Mandela did.

If we really want to be better, our critics are our most valuable assets. Haters are not critics. Haters are not to be trusted or believed. Haters will try to bring you down in many different ways, like by spreading rumours about you. Your haters never wanted to see success in your life. Critics will find your weaknesses.

On the other hand, critics are the best because they point out your flaws. The faster you figure it out, the more you become your best self. What we need to improve in life is often revealed by constructive criticism. But some people did not like being criticized by others. They don't want to hear anything negative about their character.

Adi Shankaracharya, the renowned Advaita-Vedanta philosopher, said MAYA (illusion) covers the whole world. Today, it's becoming more evident as social media is a new age "MAYA". Surrounded by notifications, this is exactly what social media is doing in our lives. If you are a user of any social media, then you may have come across the feeling of FOMO (fear of missing out). You always feel like you have nothing and you're not good enough. You think you are not cool enough to fit in with social trends. You will always be hurt by any of these things. This will not in any way improve your life.

According to an old proverb, you are the average of the five individuals you spend the most time with. But today, it is not only with whom you spend time but also what type of content you are consuming on social media that will dictate your life. A recent study shows that our time on social media negatively affects our lives.

People spend about three hours a day on social media, on average. Millions of influencers can get inside your head and convince you to follow them. It is harmful to you as well as to our society at large. If we do not limit our time on social media, our lives will become a complete mess. If social media ruins your life, you can't sue Mark Zuckerberg or any Internet company. It is your fault. This is why the term "social media diet" (limiting social media usage or deactivating social media accounts) has become more popular nowadays.

Monotonous living makes our daily lives uninteresting. But there is a way to get away from this. Make a list of the things that makes you happy, such as pets, food, travelling, hiking, driving, painting, photography, acting, dancing, and so on. Find time to do it regularly. Do it both quantitatively and qualitatively, and measure the improvements.

Life is a process of change, whether you like it or not. If you don't change on your own, don't worry, time will do it for you. But if you allow time to change you, your life will be extremely challenging because you'll be forced to change.

There are three types of people when it comes to change: those who think they are perfect and never try to change are very sceptical and overconfident.

The second type is people who think they have a problem but don't want to change anything because they are happy where they are and don't want to leave their comfort zone. They are afraid that making any changes will upset their normal lives.

The third type is people who are always ready for changes because they know they can't expect any progress if nothing changes.

The happiness index of our country is going down. In 2013, we were at number 111, but now we are at 139 out of 157 countries. Isn't it pretty bad? Happiness does come from interpersonal relationships. If happiness comes from relationships with other people, then the higher the population, the greater the happiness. If that were the case, our country would rank first because we are the most populous country. On the contrary, we have the world's lowest levels of happiness.

Why? We still don't know how to work well together. We hate people more than we love them. There are more reasons to hate someone than to love them. People are treated unfairly because of their country, religion, caste, colour, social status, wealth, and education.

We are not living in an era of depression and poverty. We are living in a better time in human history. In the last few decades, we eliminated poverty to its maximum extent. 85% of the population lives in developed countries. Facts and data show us our world is getting much better now. Fake news, corrupted politicians, and bad economic policies worsen our lives.

A 22-year-old study shows that people who think about their priorities and goals most of the time will achieve what they are looking for. Unsuccessful people usually think about the people they don't like, the events they hate, and the environment they don't want. They try to blame everyone in any given situation.

If we spend too much time with negative people, we will lose the ability to find the positive in any circumstance. Consequently, we will constantly think negatively. Getting rid of every negative friend from your circle is the best way to safeguard your future.

I am sure you have heard the story of Mowgli, a human boy who is raised by wolves in the forest. The same thing will happen if you spend your time with negative people. You will become one of them if you stay with them, there is no doubt about that. Eventually, you will start to believe negative things are the right things and defend negativity all your life.

The opposite of positivity is negativity. Negative people are self-destroyers and destroy others no matter if they are your friends or relatives.

Every thought unconsciously favours negativity. For example, if you think that you must be better than everyone else, it means you want everyone else to be behind you, technically. That in itself is a negative statement. You will continue to do what you want regardless of what others feel. But if you say, I want to improve myself, that is a positive statement. Because it will force you to do good things every day. If any of your thoughts have a negative side, you will never become a positive person.

It is difficult to cultivate positive emotions, and when we do, it feels like we force ourselves to become positive beings. This is one of the reasons we don't think that positivity is the way forward.

Studies have shown that people tend to believe bad news is true. If I tell you our country will become a superpower within the next five years, you might not believe me. But if I told you our country is going to lose millions of jobs in the next few months without any proof, you would believe that it is true. It is due to our evolutionary history. From an evolutionary point of view, when we were insignificant creatures, we had to focus on threats to survive.

Make the most of the day by talking to yourself in positive words. When you speak, you not only utter the words but also hear what you're saying. The more you speak negatively, the more likely you are to believe it. Our brain is unable to distinguish between what is right and wrong for us. If you constantly put yourself down and speak negatively to yourself, you will attract terrible experiences to you.

Why couldn't we ever forgive someone who insulted us just once? We will never forgive someone, no matter how long we have been with them, until the day we feel broken. We keep thinking of the negative side rather than the positive side. Research shows that negative events have a bigger effect than positive ones.

Our days are consumed by reacting to trivial matters. Time spent reacting is time not spent on what needs to be done. In any given situation, how we react is also an important factor in our well-being. Your response in a given circumstance should not be determined by how you feel about it; instead, you should focus on realizing how to respond in a way that is acceptable to the situation and does not cause harm to anybody else.

We should always be thankful for this life, no matter what it is. Cultivating the habit of being grateful for every good thing that gives us a positive experience; we should also be grateful for the bad things in life because they taught us valuable lessons. There is also a neurological reason behind gratitude. When we practice gratitude, it has a longer-lasting effect on staying positive than any other method. The more positive thoughts you have in a day, the faster your life will transform.

I think our culture teaches us to have more superstitious ideas about fate, destiny, and other things. It's okay to have beliefs, but what if they stop us from making efforts to move forward? We believe that what happened to us was meant to happen, and that statement makes us feel better. We don't want to be responsible for what went wrong. Many poor people think that they were born poor because of bad karma from their past lives and have to stay poor for the rest of their lives. But once we get out of this fate box, we will do a lot to improve our lives.

There is an idea called the Swedish Art of Death Cleaning. It means if we get rid of some of our abundance, our lives will become more peaceful. People who are obsessed with acquiring more material possessions are more likely to be anxious, depressed, and have low self-esteem.

Minimalism is now a powerful way to live a more meaningful life. We possess many things that we don't need. Online marketing is so addicting that we have to force ourselves to buy it. Less is always good. When we think of less, we think of limiting our desires, possessions, assets, expectations, and worries.

Now, we are aware that every purchase has an effect on the environment. When purchasing a new pair of jeans, you should be aware that each pair requires 8,000 litres of water. Consider the other side of the story on the worldwide depletion of water resources. In the past, we have never fought over water, but that could change in the future. It is even possible for states within a country to wage war for water.

Tomorrow, we will witness a widespread anti-materialist movement. The more we own, the more we leave a mark on our environment. Minimalism is the new way to live in harmony with nature. The minimalist point of view advises us to clear out our workspace, our house, our minds, and even our friends.

Positivity is contagious. People who love your presence will stay with you. People who respect you want to stay with you. Have you noticed that it feels better when certain people walk into a room? If you want to become one of those people, you should try to become a positive person.

I'd like to share a story that happened just recently. Many foreigners, especially Europeans, come to my neighbourhood to learn yoga. They are coming here to become certified yoga teachers. One day, out of nowhere, three little puppies showed up. They were only a month or two months old. They were alone, and it is likely that their mother had left them after giving birth. One day, a young European woman began to feed them. She gave them food and water every day without any reservation. Before that, no one really cared about the puppies. After almost a week, many people started giving them food and water. This is how being positive can change the world around us. If you lead by example and do good things, others will follow.

When you see a worker just walking into the factory, ask him, "How are you?" Tell him, "You look fantastic today, and your dress looks great." These words may have a ripple effect on their performance. Having such daily good habits makes a workplace a happy place.

The way we live is a reflection of our focus. Positive psychology promises to improve the quality of life. A positive person contains hope and the ability to find positivity even in the worst situation.

If you can eliminate the "I can't" word from your life for the next five years, you will become a more accomplished person.

The only thing we'll ever regret is the good times we didn't spend with our families and friends. No one will be proud of buying three houses and five cars on their deathbed; instead, we will regret buying many things that never make us happy rather than focus on the things that matter.

Do not correlate your emotions with negative words. If you find yourself having negative thoughts, simply replace them with positive ones. For example, if you feel sad, you never say, "I am sad." Instead, you should say, "I feel low happiness." Then you will experience peace in grief. When you're feeling down, consider things from a different angle. There is always a positive aspect to every situation. Reframe your feelings. You'll feel much better.

Negative statement	Positive statement
This job is unpleasant for me	How will my life be different if I do my job better than other people?
My boss is abusive	Now I can handle any kind of criticism, so I can do my job stress-free.
I have bad debt	Due to my debt, I am able to manage my expenses and save more.
I was born poor	If I work hard, I can make a fortune on my own, and then my success story will inspire many people.
I have no prestigious university education	Working hard and being competent is more valuable than having a degree.
I am a failure	I have learned a most valuable lesson

In the same way, you can turn any negative statement into a positive one. These statements will have a more significant effect on your life than you think.

"Can you control your future?" the answer is no. "Can you control what's going on?" No. "Can you live a stress-free life?" No. "Can you live problem-free life?" No. "Can you live a life without failure?" No. "Can you live a life without conflicts?" No. However, you have complete control over your habits, emotions, reactions, network, and perspective. Since more than 80 percent of your life is under your control, why are you concerned about the remaining 20 percent?

It doesn't mean that a positive attitude will always get us a successful life. The efforts that make no progress should be given up. Life always has ups and downs. How we handle our ups and downs is determined by how much control we have over our lives.

Expecting a negative outcome is also very important, just like having a Plan B. It is known as "negative visualization" in Stoic philosophy. It can help you overcome your fears and unnecessary worries. It helps you to calculate how much risk is involved in the process. Before starting any project, it is good to ask how many ways it can fail.

Negative situations and negative feedback will guide you in identifying the blind spots in your business. It is more important to know how to deal with bad situations than to anticipate only favourable ones. The problem is we trust only a few of our employees, and we expect to be happy only in certain situations. Both carry a substantial possibility of disastrous outcomes.

How does it look like a positive person? They uphold good values, work hard, are optimistic, are content, and are grateful for everything. They are more caring and confident. They are humble and patient. They keep others happy. A positive person in a company reduce stress and improve teamwork, loyalty, and relationship.

Do you have any idea why certain people are always happy? Because they have earned it. Nothing comes your way unless you work for it. Each day of their life, they accomplish something. They cherish their relationships. They love what they do. They are so involved in their day that they forget to complain and blame others. They believe they are worthy of every second of life.

Willpower: Miracle

"Where there is a will, there is a way", have you heard this proverb? Willpower is the capacity to overcome our immediate appreciation to pursue long-term objectives. Our willpower is the single most important factor in determining our success.

In 1972, Stanford University psychologist Walter Mischel and his colleagues conducted research on delayed gratification, which later became the famous "Marshmallow Test" for kids. In the study, kids were offered a single marshmallow if they wanted to have it immediately or two marshmallows if they waited for the researchers to return. In a follow-up study, the researchers found that the children who waited a long time for a reward proved to have better life outcomes, such as higher SAT scores, a healthier BMI, and enhanced social skills, than the children who opted for instant gratification.

If we don't pursue immediate benefits, we develop the ability to delay gratification and can focus on long-term achievements. This topic has been the focus of a number of experiments and research. All of them arrived at the same conclusion: a person who can stay in control in the present has a greater chance of living a successful life.

As a result, it's clear that having strong willpower is crucial for our well-being under any conditions. But just having strong willpower won't help you get better.

According to the study, one's willpower is typically greater when pursuing a long-term goal. If your motive is to make more money in the short term, for example, you will not run a successful business but rather one with lower expenses. You will cut costs from the corner, you will work with below-average employees, you will not care about systems and standards, you will not invest, and you will never focus on the future and competition. But if you are motivated by a higher cause, you may build a business where everyone aspires to work and collaborate.

A lack of willpower is the greatest hindrance to bettering our lives. If we give in to any temptation in life, it could eventually lead to addiction. In a nutshell, addiction is the loss of control over one's life. The majority of people who are addicted to drugs or alcohol commit suicide because they lack the willpower to quit their habit and are forced to do so.

Next time you ask an alcohol addict how they feel about drinking. They will tell you how miserable they are and how they wish they could get out of this addiction but don't know how. The decrease in willpower in our everyday lives may impair our ability to resist temptations.

Self-discipline, routine, habits, and diet are all important parts of keeping our willpower up all day. When we have full control over ourselves, we start making real progress.

Self-control is the most important factor in fostering strong willpower. Developing self-control involves more than just practicing resistance. We require a sense of purpose and direction in life. The primary obstacles to our self-control are temptations. We must understand how to avoid temptations. But some studies show that limiting temptations doesn't make a big difference in how strong our willpower is. To make long-term changes in your life, you also need a compelling reason.

For example, assume you eat a hamburger from McDonald's every day. Let's say you drive to work every day and pass a McDonald's outlet where you eat every day. You wished to break your binge-eating habit. Now you're working on your temptations and building up your willpower. Every time you pass McDonald's on that route, you remind yourself, "I don't want to eat that anymore."

In this circumstance, though, you regularly deplete your willpower reserves. Eventually, one day, you will go and eat it. Change your route so that there are no fast-food restaurants along the way, and adopt the habit of a healthy lifestyle. The ideal method is to create an environment where temptations are consciously forgotten. At first, you use a great deal of effort to resist the desire to consume fast food. After a while, it becomes a habit, and you no longer need to exert your willpower reserves to avoid the food.

We all want to indulge in immediate pleasure and enjoyment. The ability to self-control is the key to staying away from all those distractions. Imagine a world full of people who are not under their control; the crime rate would reach one hundred percent. It's impossible to find somebody who isn't drinking or smoking. You will not see a wealthy person or a well-educated person. You cannot imagine a home without conflicts or a world without war. You'll never see someone who is happy or peaceful. Without self-control, our lives devolve into total chaos.

We can strengthen our willpower by learning to delay immediate gratification. What is the most efficient way to exercise delayed gratification? To begin with, recognize and steadily build your responsibility. We often deny, blame, and lack a sense of responsibility. If you put off watching your favorite Netflix show so you can finish your homework, you will gain more from your assignment.

As a student, it's your responsibility to study hard. But when parents tell their kids to study, they often get mad because they wish to watch their favorite movies and online shows. Likewise, as an employee, it is your obligation to improve your performance and results, not to please your boss or involve yourself in office politics.

Not only does the practice of self-discipline and self-control develop willpower, but also the food we consume. Our brain accounts for just 1/50th of our body mass yet uses 1/5th of the calories we consume. The majority of conscious processes occur in our prefrontal cortex, which is the area of our brain responsible for attention, short-term memory, problem-solving, and impulse control. It is what distinguishes us as humans.

A comprehensive analysis of advanced research has proven the correlation between nutrition and willpower. Researchers assigned to tasks that required willpower saw a significant decrease in blood glucose levels. Therefore, it is crucially important to consume more brain foods to strengthen our willpower. Complex carbohydrates and proteins, which keep the blood sugar level steady for a long time, are the foods that high achievers choose to eat.

The only thing that can make or break a person is their habits. According to a study by Duke University, forty percent of our daily actions are not decisions but habits. Our habits play an important role in strengthening our willpower. Pick the best habits that keep you from giving in to temptation. Set habits that establish personal and professional priorities and develop a genuine interest in something you're truly passionate about. In one of the studies, even the patterns in the brain were found to be influenced by our habits.

A good habit can profoundly change one's life. Last year, one of my friends started going to the gym. His goal for the new year was to get six-pack abs in the next six months. At the end of the eighth month, he made it. Since then, everything in his life has transformed substantially. Now, he believes anything is possible if you work hard and don't give up. Before that, he was extremely feckless and spent all his time watching Netflix and playing video games.

When he started taking care of his body, he began eating only nutritious foods. He now gets up early every day. He begins to read books. He is now 1,000 times more productive at work than he used to be. He is not wasting his time on unnecessary things. He is more focused on the quality of his life. Today, he is happier and more tranquil.

He once asked me, "Why did I start working out so late in life?" He also said he felt like he could have accomplished a lot more if he had started the good habits earlier in life. This is the power of good habits: if one good habit is formed, many more good habits will follow effortlessly.

What if you are a smoker? Would you think that I should have started smoking much earlier? Negative habits drag you down not only physically but also mentally and emotionally.

We've all seen that Steve Jobs always wears the same style of clothes. He wears the same color T-shirt, pants, and sneakers every day. We've seen Mark Zuckerberg, Albert Einstein, Barack Obama, Giorgio Armani, and many other famous people dressed this way. Why do they choose to dress like that?

They are not physically attracted to that color or style of clothing, but there is a solid scientific justification for it. They're seeking to avert the onset of a syndrome called "decision fatigue." These ultra-rich celebrities feel they must stay more alert to maintain their energy levels throughout the day. Each day, we make tens of thousands of small and big decisions. Drink coffee or tea? Dress formally or casually? Resign the company or stay? Eating fast food or healthy food? We make countless decisions from the time we wake up in the morning until we go to bed at night. I mean, what if they make a mistake? Their single mistake has the potential to cost billions of dollars and affect millions of jobs around the globe.

The term "decision fatigue" refers to the idea that the more decisions we make, the less effective the solutions will be. Finally, we will make terrible decisions. We, as humans, have a very limited capacity to regulate our behavior. Evidence shows that individuals experiencing decision fatigue are not good at making the right choices. A company's success hinges on its leaders' ability to make rational decisions.

Judges have also been investigated to determine if they suffer from decision fatigue. It showed the percentage of favorable rulings by judges on parole boards in prison dropped drastically in the morning session and increased by the evening. Judges, at the end of the day, make bad decisions. The same study was conducted with healthcare professionals and police officers, and the result was almost the same. The greater the number of decisions we make in a day, the less effective they become. Decision fatigue impairs our cognitive ability and the behavioral and psychological aspects of life.

We may overcome decision fatigue by developing a routine. You must fix a schedule for a full day in advance. As soon as you awake, set a routine that eliminates the necessity for decision-making. Set up a routine where you get up at 5 a.m., drink a cup of lukewarm water, work out for thirty minutes, read for thirty minutes, eat a healthy breakfast, and then start your work. Set priorities and work on them. When you return from the office, take a shower, take a thirty-minute walk, prepare for the following day, analyse your day, and so on. Once you've established routines in your life, you'll be able to make fewer decisions and concentrate on what matters most.

Sometimes in life, it's hard to figure out what to do. Since we can't predict what will happen, we all go for the option that promises the most immediate payoff. Willpower is the willingness to achieve your long-term goal and push yourself to take action.

Due to a lack of willpower, many of us fail to maintain good health. Many people fail to improve their careers because of a lack of willpower. Many people do not get good scores in their exams because of a lack of willpower. Willpower stands above all your skills, talents, abilities, and qualifications.

Through tapas and austerity, our ancestors developed a strong sense of self-control. There are five Niyamas in Patanjali's yoga sutra: Saucha (cleanliness), Santhosha (contentment), Tapas (austerity), Svadhyaya (self-study), and Isvarapranidhana (surrender to higher consciousness). If you can follow these five Niyama's in your daily life, it is easy to improve your willpower.

All that's stopping you from achieving your long-term goals is your willpower. Your future will be better and brighter if you practice self-control. The easiest way to save your willpower is to create situations where it is not needed. If you are always put in situations that require a lot of willpower, it won't help you in the long run.

Make a note of whatever you struggled with today that forced you to use your willpower, and fix it immediately to conserve it.

Good things come to those who wait.

Productivity: A Mistake Proof Tool

According to the most recent global study, just 12% of employees are productive in the workplace. This means if you are running your operations with 100 employees, the 90% result comes from very few of your employees (However, this percentage will, once again, go down significantly in small businesses). This is because of poor performance, unproductive tasks, and workplace interruptions.

Workers are constantly subjected to a rigorous work environment and unsupportive management, which leads to poor performance. The study also reveals that the most productive workers are those who can properly balance their personal and professional lives. A person who is dissatisfied with their personal life will find it difficult to be successful in their career, and vice versa.

Doing something vs doing something good is a huge distinction. Despite what it may seem, just because something is challenging does not mean it is right. As soon as we identify the positive qualities of our job, good outcomes will follow. Improved productivity, not rapid expansion, is the key to success.

Most small business managers, I've found in my research, are more concerned with meeting their monthly delivery schedule than with increasing efficiency. They care least about the strategy for higher efficiency or the productivity-to-headcount ratio. We shouldn't just measure productivity in terms of output but also product quality, lower cost, and timely delivery.

One of the best books written on productivity is Deep Work by Cal Newport. In this book, the author mentions three types of people who will survive in the future. They are,

- Those who have lots of money to invest
- Those who are very good with technology
- Ability to do deep work

The rest of the people are just average types who will have a hard time in the future.

The third point: The ability to do deep work, which will propel you to the top of your career. It is the highest form of productivity. Once you master this skill, you will become indispensable.

The best way to end your day more productively is to know the one thing that will make all of your other tasks easier, if you do it now. However, the majority of us do not know what the most important thing to do is. The important task doesn't mean that it will keep you busy, but it will make you more productive.

When you ask a lot of questions, it's easy to figure out what's most important. Asking questions must be a priority to improve productivity. A good employee always asks questions. Ask yourself questions all the time about the work, system, quality, people, output, and method. By the time you've asked your 100th question, you'll have accomplished more than everybody else combined.

What would make my work of higher quality? How do I identify and eliminate all the waste in the process? How many blind spots do we have? These are the few crucial questions everyone should ask to increase workplace productivity. When you avoid asking questions, you never accept reality. Acceptance builds productivity. Many of us are unwilling to acknowledge the truth. Why can't you accept the conditions that have already been proven successful?

There are three factors that affect productivity at a company level: Planning, Execution, and Contribution. In simple words, planning needs to be done at a system and process level, execution needs a good strategy, and contribution should be measured at an individual level.

In my experience with many companies, most of them do their planning at the employee level. He will do the production, he will do the inspection, he will do the dispatch, and he will do the meeting, and so on. This is where the majority of the issue arises. Work is planned at the employee level when it ought to be planned at the system and process levels. Without planning at the system and process levels, it will be impossible to measure progress.

For example, you need to deliver a hundred more products this month than usual. From my experience, I have seen many managers push employees to work more; they never try to plan for the excess quantity at a process or system level.

Execution needs experience, a proven framework, broad knowledge, and creative capacity. A company outperforms its competitors when it executes the best tactics. Superior work requires a significant level of execution.

Finally, the talent pool is the source of the contribution. The contribution factor will depend on how many of your workers truly enjoy their work. When we are unable to improve these three factors, productivity suffers at the company level.

Today is the era of smart work. We should know what is called "smart work." How do we recognize smart work? Hard work means more actions toward the goal, whereas smart work focuses on a few important actions to get more results. Smart work is a well-thought-out, time-consuming task that can be deconstructed into smaller segments, setting priorities, removing all possible errors and barriers, and completed quickly and accurately.

For example, there are two ways to remove a screw from a wooden log. Either we exert our full physical effort (hard work) or use an electric hammer (smart work). Electric hammers save 99 percent of the time and effort required. In today's industry standard, if you believe in hard work, you will not see results for a very long time. You need to train your employees to adopt smart working methods to increase productivity.

When we talk about priorities, many people are unsure how to set them. A company should set priorities based on responsibilities, commitments, and goals. When we do this, we will prioritize the most important tasks; otherwise, we will be busy with time-consuming tasks that have nothing to do with productivity.

Smart working mode activates when there are no distractions. Working is not just doing the job; it is delivering all your commitments at an acceptable quality and quantity level at the lowest cost possible. The rest is just trying to do what needs to be done and will always end up with lower satisfaction.

Setting and achieving goals is what we need to become more productive. At least three goals should be set every year to help us get more done. Without goals, the organization cannot realize its full potential. Without competence, however, achieving goals is difficult. If your company has only ordinary talents, it will be hard to hit your goals. It is easy to set reasonable goals and achieve them if we can forecast our capabilities.

According to many studies, Employees' productivity is proportional to their level of happiness. Several big corporations, such as Google and many other companies, have increased their investment in employee assistance in recent years, resulting in a 37% increase in employee productivity. Google has a C.C.O. (Chief Culture Officer) to keep all Googlers happy. Factors like health and safety, training and development, cultural diversity, human rights, and labour laws were all taken into account when developing a better work culture.

Researchers also found that companies with better scores on employee friendliness have higher returns on assets than those with lower scores on staff friendliness.

To finish a job, we must have control of three things: time, effort, and resources. We often allocate time without understanding the effort. We often fail to utilize our resources at their maximum level or we lack relevant efficient resources. We don't have enough time or money to do everything. We must decide where to invest our money and time among all the given options.

Operations are considered inefficient if you do not utilize the resources at their maximum capacity. Connecting these three dots in an extremely low friction state is the best framework for productivity. Applying new ideas or expanding ideas in more efficient ways will improve operational excellence.

Measuring productivity should focus on overall capabilities rather than a single cost set. Lower input costs are an advantage, but that isn't considered the main advantage. The objective of productivity is to produce more output per worker hour, per machine, or per tonne of raw material.

It is easy to increase the productivity of one factor by replacing it with another. For example, when you work overtime, the output per machine goes up, but this is not considered an increase in productivity. (Researchers say overtime is associated with poor management, poor control, and poor planning).

To improve productivity, improve both effectiveness and efficiency. Effectiveness means finishing the job by the deadline, whereas efficiency means finishing the job with fewer resources. Effectiveness is doing the right task, and efficiency is doing it the right way. Most order qualifiers provide the best delivery on time with cost-effective options, ensuring that customers continue to benefit from and trust them. Efficiency comes when we do things mindfully and with more clarity.

"More generates more results" is a busted theory if "more" means things that do not matter or multiple things that produce no value. Working an extra hour isn't a big deal, but if you keep working five or six extra hours for the long term, you won't get as much out of it. There will be no one interested in working with you if this is how you manage your company. Because employees don't feel they achieved more; rather, they feel more stressed and demotivated.

This phenomenon is called diminishing returns, where more input yields less progress. Increasing the factor of production does not always lead to increased marginal productivity. The efficiency is constrained by many other factors. This means in a production process, as a production factor (labour, machine hours, and raw materials) increases, the total output will increase. Still, it will reach the optimal output level before it begins to diminish.

Have you heard the term "deliberate practice"? What distinguishes experts from the rest is deliberate practice. Every single practice needs a purpose when you perform the deliberate practice. Like in yoga, improve with purpose. Deliberate practice is a special type of practice that is purposeful and systematic. Regular practice is mindless repetition, whereas deliberate practice is focused on conscious repetition to achieve specific goals.

Deliberate practice cannot begin without first establishing clear and specific goals. It is not trying a more difficult technique but rather a different method. It's not about maxing out one's capabilities but rather growing into them.

We now have more scientific evidence to support the idea that we can learn any skill. Our brains themselves can be rewired to learn a new skill with consistent, daily practice. Without practice, talent is useless. This is why many professionals often say I am extremely talented but a failure because I am unable to accomplish anything.

The journey from the craft production method to industry 4.0 was long and interesting. Many things have changed, including the way we work, the way we consume, the way we travel, the way we communicate, the way we eat, the way we live, and the way we think. High productivity has made it possible for us to afford many things today.

If you are not a productive employee, you are still in the craft production era, which is a hundred-year-old work format.

Every process has constraints. We reached a high level of productivity when we understood and eliminated the constraints of a work process— identifying constraints that affect productivity and thinking about how to exploit those constraints in the best possible way to get good results, whether it is a man, machine, method, or material.

In many companies, the standards are based on the experience of the top executives. A manager who is secure in their own knowledge base is less likely to consider an employee's new ideas or suggestions.

A belief system based on science, innovation, evidence, and research is better than one based only on personal experience. You shouldn't just use your own experiences and information to form your beliefs. Don't be afraid to let go of long-held ideas that are holding you and your company back.

There is no 100% productivity, but it is always possible to improve your efficiency. When you can scale your work, you can scale your business.

To put it simply, when we remove the waste from the input, we get a better result. But if team performance is poor, identify and eliminate waste can be challenging. Productivity will be at its highest level if people have a good work ethic, good habits, good organizational behaviour, a workplace without distractions, the right goals and objectives, the right system and standards, and the ability to focus for the long term.

To attain exponential growth, we must persevere in accomplishing things that are at least ten times higher than what we are doing now or what our competitors are doing. Every aspect of a business requires progress, not merely survival-oriented changes.

Cost Management: For Better Today and Tomorrow

Recently, Ramu was promoted to general manager in a small production company. He felt so glad. He was employed there for nearly two decades, and his sincerity and commitment influenced his employer's decision to promote him. Unfortunately, his employer ignored to assess if he was qualified to oversee the business.

After his promotion, Ramu initiated the reward program. Whoever achieves the target will receive incentives. And the target was placed in line with the delivery schedule. It was initially intended for supervisors and engineers. Although their income exceeds that of the operators there, Ramu thought, why not give incentives only to the operators? They work harder than anyone else. Therefore, he discontinued incentives to supervisors and engineers and began giving them to operators.

There was something that went wrong. Output decreased sharply of a sudden. On the shop floor, quality issues and many new challenges arose. There he realized supervisors and engineers lost their interest in working hard. They felt discouraged by the decision. They argued managers valued operators more than them. A huge misunderstanding increased in the company. Finally, Ramu had to discontinue the incentive program. Instead of aiming for the better, it went worse and lowered productivity.

Ramu should be aware that rewards should be paid out of additional revenue; they should not cost the business. To give incentives, we should know what our actual and additional capacity is. Within the capacity giving incentives is a bad idea. Whoever contributes to the progress of your company should be rewarded for their efforts. Ramu was just assuming things would go right, but something went worst. In a small company, if you are thinking about money, think about it hundred times; it is the moral of the story.

It is impossible to summarize cost management in a few words because accounting is a vast topic. Therefore, I will emphasize the most important facets of the costing.

Managing costs helps businesses in two ways: staying competitive and increasing profitability. When we manage our costs, we will maximize predictability. Before we manage costs, we should know what kinds of costs a company has to bear to make a product or service. There are mainly two types of costs: operational and investment costs. Operational costs consist of both fixed and variable costs.

Fixed costs, in a simple definition, are the costs that are incurred regardless of how much a company produces. For example, your rent, government fees, equipment costs, and so on.

The fewer the fixed cost, the fewer we have to sell to reach the break-even point. (break-even point is a level of output at which the cost of production equals revenue). The Break-even point is equal to fixed costs/unit selling price - unit variable costs. You are at risk unless you reach your B.E.P. as quickly as possible.

Variable costs are expenses that vary proportionally with output. For example, variable costs increase as output increases and vice versa. Variable costs include raw materials, direct labour, inventory, and so on.

When there are fewer variable costs, the break-even point is reached quickly. If we can keep our variable expenses down at a given selling price, we'll make a bigger contribution to the bottom line.

In the above story, Ramu messed with the variable cost. He increased the variable costs without a proper measure, causing the company to suffer losses.

To make it easier to recognize, create a graph in which the X-axis represents total production and the Y-axis represents the costs incurred. You will see the variable costs are proportional to production, while fixed costs are independent of production.

By analysing fixed and variable costs, a business can determine whether to invest in plants, equipment, or properties relative to the volume of the production and the volatility.

Like the break-even point, return on investment is also an important measure we should consider. Every investment you make should be considered an asset, and it should pay off many times over. Return on investment is a measure that shows if your performance is getting better over time or worse. R.O.I. is the best reference point to manage your costs.

Operating costs are ordinarily under your control. The greater your level of control, the more competitive you become.

We assume that we will keep trading in the same way forever. Therefore, we perceive the change less seriously. Consequently, we are unwilling to invest in change. The best investment cost is to invest in the revolution.

Costs, selling prices, and profits are linked together. You always need the plan to defend your selling price by emphasizing how much better your product or service is than the competition. You cannot sell anything without purchasing raw materials, paying rent and wages, as well as equipment and maintenance costs. The more you sell, the more it costs.

There is also a depreciation cost. Your assets are being consumed. If you consider it or not, it is happening right now. Furthermore, there are hidden costs about which we are not concerned. Like all the other costs, even hidden costs can be measured. Here is one good example.

Ramu, the general manager of a production company, conducts a meeting every morning from 9 to 9.30 a.m. It has been going on for the past five years. His company earns almost twenty crores every year. Let's do a useful calculation: If he spends thirty minutes a day in a meeting, that's three hours a week, twelve hours a month, and six days a year. Let's do the math for five years. The annual revenue is 20 crores or approximately 6 lakhs per day. The company lost about 1.80 crore rupees over a period of five years because of the daily meeting. This was the hidden cost that Ramu incurred for the company.

The purpose of a meeting should be to analyse what your team achieved last month. How many problems have been solved yet? What has been accomplished, and what remains unaccomplished? What are the plans for the short term and long term? Not more than this, and meetings should not be held each day but once a month, and they should be less than thirty minutes. An effective meeting includes everyone's participation, appreciation for the good work, and opportunities for feedback and key decisions. Employees are certainly unproductive if your business can't operate without a daily meeting.

There are a lot of hidden costs that you can avoid if you care about cost management. Hidden costs will also happen when you try to cut costs instead of managing them.

I personally know many small companies are not doing calibration of their equipment on time, not filling the fire extinguisher, not investing in technology for higher productivity, not spending money on replacement or maintenance, not having a training program, or downsizing their workforce are not effective ways to improve the bottom line.

For example, downsizing your workforce eventually results in low morale, and your employees will invest less effort. Cost cutting on manpower is a counter-productive strategy, as per research. Most downsizing strategies do not work as intended. Non-downsized companies perform well than downsized companies as per the research. You always need the best to function at the peak, not the cheapest. Do not cut costs where it affects performance or productivity.

I know of a company that bought its own space many years ago. Despite the growth, they had no plans to relocate to a larger facility. The machines are congested, leaving no space for proper maintenance. They can actually rent their space and relocate to a better location. To save money, they are destroying their productivity. Can it be considered a hidden cost? Most likely, yes.

We must have a good understanding of which areas are affected by the cost. Know the nature of your expenses, such as where your costs are the highest, why it is less profitable, where you should discourage and reduce costs, and how costs are increasing. Perspective is what makes cost management possible.

There are many risks that come with doing business, but the cost is on the top. If you do not control your costs, you will be forced to deal with them every day, which is not practical. If you don't manage your costs well, it will drag your business down.

We must teach our employees the fundamentals and the importance of cost management to reduce the cost of each department. For example, instruct your office assistant how to save sugar, tea bag, or coffee powder to control costs on beverages. Such as limiting tea timings, reducing wastage, and switching off the machines. Only a shared approach will work. Effective cost management is predicated on inclusiveness.

Operational efficiency is an important measure of managing costs. According to studies, unit costs decreased by a constant and predictable amount if the cumulative volume of a task doubled. This will only work when you can make the process faster, when you can use more efficient materials and machines, and when all your technical problems are solved.

When your operational efficacy increases, your capital costs per dollar of sales will be much better than those of your competitors. Always consider taking your operational costs less cost-effective compared to last year.

You can reduce your spending on everything, including energy savings on utilities, removing redundant roles, outsourcing, and leveraging the Internet.

For instance, consider transportation. Correct tyre pressure, slower acceleration, and a half-full tank increase savings by 10%. Also, using oil cards and greener vehicles will reduce your transportation costs.

In normal conditions, we should control costs in one direction, and in a crisis, in the opposite direction. Imagine you are employed and have a family to care for. You effectively manage your expenses. What would you do if you lost your job unexpectedly? You should really cut costs than managing it.

A crisis doesn't mean that there has to be a recession; even if you are threatened by competition, losing consumers, or your future is uncertain, you are experiencing a crisis.

A small company is always good because there are fewer people, which means less space, less equipment, fewer wages, less working capital, and so on.

You must have a budget every year. Targets in the budget should be realistic and achievable. A budget is intended for those who are accountable for the results. For example, let the people in charge of production prepare the budget for production.

Let's say a monitor in a machine keeps breaking down. Instead of doing maintenance, replace it. If the production team requires new software that can reduce effort and monitor production in real-time, then it is a good idea. However, an exact prognosis is required, such as the possibility that new software will reduce effort by 50 percent.

The more often you look over your costs, the more ways you will find to keep track. Priorities for cost-cutting must be established, as it is impossible to achieve everything at once.

All small businesses can make a profit each year by either cost management or improved productivity. Increasing sales and new product launches are always difficult.

Distraction: Free Pass To Hell

Ramu and Raju were neighbours. Both were of the same age and went to the same elementary school, high school, and college. They both applied for the same job at the same company and were hired at the same time.

Twenty years later, Ramu was promoted to C.E.O. of the company, whereas Raju remained an unnoticed shop floor worker in a small company. Today, Ramu's income is tenfold that of Raju's. How did this all happen? They both went to the same college and started working at the same time. But why is Ramu so much better off than Raju?

Let's have a look at their work history over the past twenty years. Ramu's primary goal in life is to get better at what he is doing. Every year, he wrote down specific goals and worked hard to achieve all of them. His contribution to his company was more significant than anyone else's. When needed, he stepped up to take on extra responsibilities. The relationship he built with clients, co-workers, and management was undeniable. As he moved up the corporate ladder, he spent more time learning "soft skills" like how to deal with people, how to talk to them, how to solve problems, how to think, and so on.

Due to his expertise, he has become more visible and well-known in the industry. He was available at all times, and he never said "no," "I can't," or "It's not my job." He took ownership of many challenges that others often ignored or avoided. In general, he enjoyed spending the day in his company. Because of Ramu's diligence, his company earned a solid reputation and made a substantial profit.

Going to work, in his mind, was like walking into a maze. The most successful are those who spend a lot of time and effort exploring the unknown path and finding the exit as early as possible.

On the other hand, Raju was a little off track. He was unable to add value to the firm he worked for. However, he's only there for the pay check. It made no difference to him what happened within the company. He had been noticed for the wrong reasons on several occasions. He never stayed a minute longer than his regular working hours. He's always been unhappy with his boss and co-workers.

Each day, he came up with new excuses and complaints about not being able to accomplish his work. He changed many companies over his twenty-year career. He was never a dependable worker. He was at a loss for professional direction. He never listened to his mentors or seniors. His twenty years of work experience were full of distractions.

Because they started together with the same qualification, Ramu learned how to work for a company, whereas Raju was always distracted. Ramu never stopped learning, while Raju stopped learning after college. A person's downfall begins the moment they stop learning.

Every day, we experience distraction on four levels: emotional (pleasure, sadness), psychological (our surroundings), biological (cravings), and intellectual (honour, name). To survive, we must transcend all distractions. Most business owners fail due to intellectual distractions, such as pursuing fame, wealth, power, and so forth. Management-level distractions can be eliminated if you are able to focus on value, innovation, and hard work.

By the time Dhirubhai Ambani died, the two Ambani brothers had fled to take control of the company. When their legal fight got worse, their mother, Kokila Ben, negotiated an agreement between both brothers. Mukesh Ambani took control of power, telecommunications, and financial services. Anil Ambani took control of the energy and manufacturing sectors. In the beginning, Anil outperformed his brother, Mukesh Ambani. In 2008, Anil Ambani became the sixth richest person in the world. Just twelve short years later, as he recently testified in court, his net worth is zero.

Billion dollars to zero, how did that happen? It's easy to lose sight of the forest for the trees as we climb the success ladder. Being too confident about success and legacy will distract us from what we are doing now.

Overconfidence often leads to ignoring fundamental business principles. It distracts us from everything that must be considered important. A few bad decisions, no long-term plans, over-diversification without core knowledge, massive debt, incompetence with competitors, and corruption charges brought him riches to rags.

Anything that stops us from achieving our short-term and long-term goals is a distraction. We can't be better at what we are doing if we can't improve the skills and knowledge needed for a job or a business. If your customers are dissatisfied or your company is not generating a profit, it means you are not paying attention to many aspects of your business. To prevent your company from failing, you must promptly identify and eliminate all potential sources of distraction.

But his brother Mukesh Ambani is a visionary leader. There is nothing unimportant or irrelevant that he cares about. He works harder than anyone else in his family. He never prioritizes anything that has no bearing on the company's bottom line. He only cares about one thing: taking the right actions every time. He believes it is possible to get things right the first time around. Errors cost a lot of money and reputation when you're playing for the big prize.

Anything is possible if we are not distracted from our focus. Our mind is dubbed the monkey mind. Our concentration is continuously shifting. It is hard to keep our minds under control and focus on important activities for the long term. However, the person who best handles our monkey mind is the one who earns the most rewards.

Have you ever heard of André Agassi? He was one of the greatest tennis players in history. Andre Agassi was the first male player to win each of the four Grand Slam championships on three distinct surfaces. In his autobiography "OPEN", he recounted losing a French Open final owing to his wig.

If you don't know who he is, the below picture will help you recognize him (wearing his famous wig). He was unbeatable talent throughout his tennis career, winning eight Grand Slam championships, including Wimbledon, the Australian Open, the French Open, and the US Open. He's always been a significant figure in the tennis world. Pete Sampras was his only rival.

He began to lose his hair at a very young age. His hair loss had left him depressed and unsure of his identity. He tried manydifferent methods to get his natural hair to grow, but in the end, he was disappointed with the results. He got distracted and started wearing a custom-made, very expensive wig.

It was the day before the French Open final in 1990; he was taking a shower when his wig fell apart. He panicked and called his brother to mend the situation. However it was a specially manufactured wig, which was not easy to get in a day. In that very important game, he had to wear that busted wig. André Agassi himself said that before the match, he prayed, not for the victory but for his wig not to fall off during the play. His focus was on the wig and not on the game. Finally, he lost one of the most important games.

We will never achieve what we want unless we tackle our psychological and emotional distractions. Our mental fitness is the key to getting rid of our weaknesses.

Our biggest distraction is our identity. We have fought over five thousand wars in three thousand years, including two world wars. We killed many people in the name of religion and beliefs. We further divide humanity into the poor and rich. We hate others questioning our identity. An identity crisis creates significant distress in daily life by interfering with our ability to function normally. We identify as managers and owners, yet we fail to fulfil our obligations.

Identity involves experience, beliefs, memories, relationships, and values. Those who grow up with a positive identity will face any trouble with courage. A person with a negative identity will experience more trouble throughout their life.

For Agassi, a man without hair is a sign of an unimpressive personality, particularly one who is always in the media spotlight and a world-renowned figure like him. Without hair, he felt he could be unattractive to others. This greatly distracted him, causing him to lose a grand slam championship.

When we get a promotion to manager, we often identify more with the title than with the work. This is why most managers of small businesses don't do their jobs well. When I interviewed unsuccessful managers, they all identified themselves as managers but not as responsible workers. From a worker on the shop floor to a manager, what changes is not the position but the sense of responsibility. In a company, there is no such thing as good or bad work. It shows how narrow-minded we are about our work.

Because of a sense of entitlement, many managers believe their position is the most important one, and everyone who works under them is not so important. They, therefore, make independent decisions. Finally tries to figure out what went wrong with other people. When you believe you are perfect and superior to everyone else, the problem is on your side.

We sabotage our careers due to the many outside influences that can divert our attention. Lessons from Agassi's life can illuminate the correct route. Look at another story: the dismissal of Bill Clinton, the 42nd president of the United States of America. At the age of 46, he was the third-youngest president in the country. Until then, his life was so marvellous, filled with achievements. He was a great student; he earned a scholarship to study at a university, where he met Hilary and married her in 1975.

During his tenure from 1993 to 2000 (until his indictment), he signed many famous bills that positively impacted the lives of Americans. Whether it was enlisting gays in the army or national health care reform, he did legendary work. But at the same time, his distraction began to take effect. He turned his attention to Monica Lewinsky, a trainee who later worked for the White House. This was the beginning of his extraordinary career's downfall.

He could have gotten more out of his life if that distraction had not occurred. He was a good husband, a loving father, an attorney general, an effective governor, the president of the National Association of Governors, the chairman of the Education Commission, and a two-term President of the United States. But because of his distraction, the legacy he had built over the years has been obliterated.

Distraction weakens you because it will navigate through several bad circumstances. Any intent, thought, relationship, or activity in which we experience immediate pleasure might be a source of distraction. It will eventually become a burden in life. Any activity that is morally unjustifiable can be a distraction.

All criminal acts are the secondary development of a distracted mind.

In Steven Covey's book, 7 Habits of Highly Effective People, I think we should add the eighth habit, "Traction," which is the opposite of distraction. Because despite having these seven behaviours, many people fail due to distraction. Distraction is the fastest way to feel good whereas traction means sacrifice.

We can achieve anything in this world if we put in our continuous best efforts without getting distracted. But we are all dreamers. We build castles in our dreams, not in reality. Building real castles need deliberate actions without any distractions. Those who achieve modest results exert little effort. Less distracted people think they are more productive and feel motivated.

There is an easy method for measuring employee distraction at your workplace. Assign any two workers to the same task and see who gets it done faster. Do not specify the deadline, but instruct them to do the task as quickly as feasible. They shouldn't know that they both have been given the same assignment. Those who completed the task in less time and with greater quality and detail would have experienced fewer distractions.

Practicing visualization techniques help you get away from many distractions. Try to visualize everything you did from morning to evening. Reflect on the day's events half an hour before going to bed. Honestly evaluate all the events because the only person you are honest with is you. Recollect how many hours you spend on meetings, firefighting, email replies, looking for solutions, interviewing, talking to customers, and handling people. Most of the time we spend on activities may not be on important things.

Pause often and reflect on your work. Think about taking a U-turn if you feel what is happening is not good for the organization. There are many ways to do a job. Find a way that has a simple process and is easy to execute. Pause and turn to the right path, where you can anticipate a green signal. If your process has no clarity and more complexity is bound to have many distractions.

We usually take others' time to do our job. We ask for help and assistance to finish our job. Teamwork is often misunderstood by many workers. Teamwork doesn't mean that we should work together. Work independently so that the entire value stream is improved. This is teamwork. Everyone should work on their own so that the work becomes teamwork.

A company introduced an ERP system to its operations. A few months later, they discontinued and began to work as before. This puzzled me, so I asked about it. Their explanation for discontinuing the ERP System was that everyone was hooked to their computer. No one is willing to stay on the factory floor. Many people argued technology was a distraction. If it is so, how can the world be like it today? We would still be living in a barbaric culture. Technology is helping us save time and effort, but we either overuse it or misuse it.

Do not ignore or tolerate any mistakes. The compound effect of ignorance is a failure. If you are successful today, and if you don't figure out what distractions may come your way, indeed, you are not going to achieve another success in life. Tough times are only temporary. There is always light after the darkness if we are ready to remove distractions from our life.

Our world is shaped like this today only because some people dare to do their duty without any distractions.

In the workplace, distractions are the negative habits that employees engage in. A few of the most common bad practices I noted during my research are given below.

Most small businesses revolve around one key person. This will only help that person to grow. They will try to intervene in all the jobs and consider themselves the highest authorities. Micromanaging essentially means not letting others do the work. It is wasting everyone's time. We can resolve micro-management by giving authority and freedom to all employees. Effectively implementing systems thinking, time management principles, and proper delegation will eliminate the need for micro-managing.

The practice of favouritism undermines efforts to maintain a dedicated team. Many managers have faith in a few employees who appear to work harder than others. In a company, every individual must be considered important. Instead of favouritism, you can practice meritocracy to motivate talent.

We do have plans in the paper but don't know how to effectively carry out those plans. For this reason, we are engaged in daily firefighting. Planning is the lifeline of work. Based on our plans, we need to make preparations. Preparations are just as important as planning. Planning can be written in one line, but preparations need a lot of checklists.

For example, if you are planning to climb Mount Everest, you need to do more preparation than just climbing a small hill. You need better gear, strength training, and a well-experienced team.

Most of us are afraid of taking risks. We don't need to take risks if everything is under our control and everything is favourable. But this is not the case. Most of us do not take risks because we don't know the concept of calculated risk. Taking a calculated risk means jumping from the hilltop with a parachute.

Work can be done effectively only with the help of a system. If we cannot implement a system, we cannot measure the progress. Many companies have systems in place but noactions have been taken to improve or optimize them. Optimization is the best way to speed up the process.

Selfish motives are the side effects of ego and the wrong culture. Both are detrimental to running a successful business.

Having clear goals is required to beat distractions. Most small businesses don't set short-term or long-term goals. Having no goal means having no purpose. Without a goal, nothing is achievable.

When I asked managers about their goals, many of them said that their goals were to meet the deadline and cut costs. A goal shouldn't be just to make your operations better; it should also be to serve the big picture. After all, it's up to your supervisors and workers to make the operations better. A management goal should be like building a great reputation, developing great culture, encouraging innovation, focusing on core competencies, and becoming the best in your industry.

Distraction is time spent on unproductive work. It is a huge risk you are taking if you do not take any measures to cut down on distractions from your workplace. Imagine paying a painter a large sum of money who has never made a single drawing before. You'll see they are doing their job, but since they are inexperienced with the technique, it is impossible to gauge their progress. A distraction-less work culture produces more in less time, and your work culture will continue to produce the desired results. You will never get the value that is anticipated when you are distracted at your job.

Every company should establish a distraction list (what not to do) for their employees. Workers unknowingly follow certain patterns that are full of distractions, but they will do their best if we guide them. Workplace distractions can be reduced significantly if office politics and gossip are eliminated.

Distraction will separate you from your goals, affect your career advancement, take away all your fortunes, you never seem to have enough time to get things done, impede your capacities, and always deliver low-quality results. I think more than a strategy or framework, we need the right attitude, which is required to overcome distractions.

Success and Failure: A Philosophy

Success is a philosophy; we can't define it by looking at the outcome. When you accomplish something that everyone else says is impossible, you might consider it a success. Failure is a result, but it adds fuel to our effort.

Except for humans, all other living beings reach their full potential during their lifetime. Our whole lives are spent trying to figure out what went wrong, but in reality, we're lazy, ignorant, and focused on the wrong thing.

When you've lived 100 years, you're a success compared to others who have lived less than 100 years. People believe you are successful if you have been running a company for a long time compared to those who have closed their businesses. When you graduated from IIT, you felt more successful than the others who attended a less prestigious institution. But in reality, success is indescribable, even though comparisons with others may quantify it.

Success is personal, unparalleled, and judged by the result. Success is the culmination of many goals put together to achieve the mission. It is a story built upon many sacrifices, right actions at the right time, failures, and life lessons. Thinking and acting beyond our capacity is the secret to success. It is the result of greatness and the outcome of many competitive advantages. Success is directly proportional to the value we create over time.

To become successful, first of all, we need a **"cause"**, and we should believe in that cause with our whole hearts. We need a cause that inspires us to work day and night without hesitation. Even when the odds are against us, we must continue to do what is necessary to justify the cause. If you always look for a reward, you will only be able to work in a certain way. When seeking a reward, you move in the direction where you can see the most benefits for yourself. There is no way this will lead to success.

It is the remarkable story of "mountain man" Dasarath Manjhi, who built a road through a mountain using a chisel and hammer. He was a farm worker in a tiny, underdeveloped Bihar village. His wife died after falling from the mountain in front of him while she was carrying lunch for him. He was unable to save her life since there was no road leading to the next town, and they needed to traverse a mountain to get there.

After the untimely death of his wife, he decided to build a road through the mountain so that no one would have their destiny like him. From 1959 to 1982, twenty-three years he worked nonstop, and in the end, he built a road that connected the nearest town.

How can someone break a mountain with just a chisel and hammer? If someone dedicates their life to a good cause, nothing can stop them from succeeding.

Imagine what if he was thinking, "What do I do now? I've lost everything. Who is going to cook for me? Who is going to raise my kids? If that's the case, his story would never be documented in the success pages of history. What should I do now? It was probably the question he asked himself many times. He was centred on the solution rather than thinking about his loss. That's how he found his cause. When he decided to build the road, he had already cut the mountain in his mind. The rest were just actions.

Success requires a cause greater than just our life, regardless of where we were born or who we are. The cause has the energy to ignite your mind and body. Manjhi belongs to the lowest caste in our Indian society, the Musharas, which means "rat eaters." He had never attended a formal school. He didn't travel out of his village. He had never heard of success stories before and had no idea what success meant. He never watched motivational videos to get him going.

As long as we put forth a consistent effort with the right mindset, anything is possible. Success is the kind of event in which you might spend a lifetime without expecting anything in return except the intended outcome.

He got the Padma Shri award (the fourth highest civilian award in our country), not because he built a road all by himself but because of the cause behind building the road. This 110-meter-long road is inspiring to all of us, and I believe such success stories deserve the title of wonders of the world.

"Mountain man" is certainly above every superman, spiderman, batman, and any other man from Hollywood. But unfortunately, our ideals are always wrong. This is why most of us struggle to identify the meaning of our lives.

(Why does our democratic system not work? It is because none of our politicians has a "**cause**". Why are they here, then? To have power, money, and authority. If you ask any politician, they will tell you they are here to serve you. What? We are grown up enough to know how to help ourselves; we know better than you what we need. You are here to bring prosperity to our nation; you are here for our security. You are here to stop corruption and discrimination. You are here to make our nation a great soft power. You are here to bring in investments and build great infrastructure. You are here to tackle many problems, including war, climate change, terrorism, unemployment, food security, poverty, pollution, deforestation, migration, human rights, population control, and so on. You're not here to beg for the vote. You are not here to divide our own people in order to safeguard your electoral base. If any politician has found a cause to serve our nation, they will do incredible things for our country. Unfortunately, you can't see anyone like that today).

It is not easy to find a cause. You need to open yourself up. One can only discover a cause if they are highly receptive. When someone is receptive, they can see things very clearly. Bruce Lee once said, "Life itself is a teacher if you want to listen to it".

In the book, the Book of Mirdad has a quote that explains receptivity really straightforwardly. "A thunderbolt never strikes a house except that house draws it to itself". "The house is as much to account for its ruin as the thunderbolt". Any circumstance or occurrence can render you receptive until you fully draw it in.

You become more receptive only:

When you love what you do.

When you live a life of great value.

When you read more books and listen to many new people, to widen your perspective.

When you are more empathetic.

When you reflect on your day and correct yourself.

When you can spend time alone in silence.

When you express gratitude for everything you have now.

Success is not for the person who deserves it; it is for the person who seeks it despite the struggles and hardships in life. If success is meant only for those who deserve it, then we would never have gotten independence from the British because they were better equipped and more advanced than our freedom fighters. Still, we have thrown out the Britishers and won our freedom back. The "deserving" factor is crucial to any success. To have that "deserving" factor, you have to give up many things in life. The synonym for success is sacrifice. The greater the level of sacrifice, the greater the chances of success.

We don't need to work hard just to maintain a living standard; we need to work hard for a great cause. If you are working hard for no reason, you are wasting your time, as well as others.

Our belief system plays a key role in our success. What if Manjhi believed he was helpless because he was just a labourer? Because of our belief system, most of us have not reached our full potential. We always set limits for ourselves. The majority of our beliefs are founded on our fears and insecurities.

We believe we can't find a good career since we don't have a premium school education. We believe we can't achieve much in life since we don't have any talent like successful people. We believe we will never become rich because we were born into a poor family, and so on. But, in reality, we have complete control over how we live. Today, the world is so fair, and opportunities are equally distributed.

Like a belief system, a direction is also important. We are consistently perplexed and unsure of where to go. Suppose our goal was to become an IAS officer, but when we got there, something else caught our attention. We don't know what to do after becoming an IAS officer. Because of this reason, many IAS officers have been charged with bribery and helping politicians commit corruption; instead, they should end corruption and work for the progress of our country.

It is the same everywhere. Students are eager to get into IITs, but when they get there, they don't know what to do. This is why many students kill themselves even though they attend good schools. To be successful, we must always think about the long term, not the short term. To get a clear direction, we should prioritize progress above every achievement.

Direction comes from total involvement. If you wish to become a manager, you must first evolve; preparation alone will not make you a competent manager. Do not focus on the change in positions alone, but consider how you can "evolve" with it. If you do not evolve, you will always focus on a few measures that can yield immediate benefits.

Evolve is the superlative form of change. First, the change must be accepted, and then it must be actively pursued. You will then begin to comprehend how to evolve it. Most of us never get past working on change. When you work on implementing changes, you may identify countless opportunities for improvement; this is the path to evolve. There is no going back to square one after you have evolved.

We have very little chance of becoming successful in life if we don't know ourselves better, especially in a workplace where people from different backgrounds work together. In this situation, better understanding oneself facilitates improved teamwork. We don't know what our strengths are, and that's why we're so conflicted. Your work will not bring you fulfilment unless you know what your strengths are.

If we can nurture our talent, we can make our normal lives more meaningful. This is not an idea but a law that applies everywhere. If you want to succeed at anything, whether it's your job, a relationship, a business, or anything else, you have to dedicate yourself completely. Dedication comes when you have extraordinary tenacity and commitment to your goals.

Our choices, preferences, and decisions all largely affect our lives. We live our lives based on the decisions we have made in the past. We are going to shape our future based on the decisions we make today. Directions come from the decisions we make, either consciously or unconsciously. When we make decisions based on assumptions, our results are likely to fail. The more we delay deciding on important activities, the worse the outcome will be. Do not postpone any decisions that require immediate correction.

All successful people have an earning mindset, whereas the rest all have a making mindset. "Making and earning mindsets" is what determines our long-term success.

Let's pick two hypothetical street vendors to understand these two mental models better. Ramu and Raju serve similar food items. Ramu has a "making mindset", and Raju has an "earning mindset". Ramu will buy cheap raw materials to save costs. To make more profit, Ramu will cut spending on all ingredients. While on the contrary, Raju will always try to bring high-quality food items. Raju will try to earn respect and trust of his customers. Raju will seek long-term benefits and satisfaction. The quality of Raju's food will be ten times better than Ramu's. Raju would be delighted to hear customers admire the food and recognize his hard work.

"Making mindset" people are greedy by nature. What do you do when you are greedy? You become more selfish and dishonest. It will only lead to more anxiety, despair, and stress in your life. Suppose you have an excess of one hundred rupees in your pocket. You saw a man beg for food on the road. In this situation, a greedy person would think, "Why would I give him my hard-earned money? What do I get in return? Why can't he work like others?" But a person without greed would buy him food without worrying too much about it.

Anything in excess would not give us any satisfaction in life but would rather make us feel more insecure. The excess money in your pocket will get you nothing until you help someone in need.

A making mindset person always looks for utility value in everything. A woman who was recently divorced went to an advocate for help with a land dispute. She was living alone and was reasonably well off. The advocate looted all of her money, knowing her condition well. Being broken, she eventually committed suicide. She had good intentions and wanted to fight for a real cause, but she was treated more like a commodity than a person.

We should treat other people on a human level, or else we will never be satisfied with our lives. We will continue to cheat people for our short-term benefit. People who are making-minded cannot be trusted or believed. Making-minded people have the power to impress others. But they all have fake personalities.

In pursuit of making money, there are thousands of options available. Cheating is an extreme form of making money. This is why a lot of well-known entrepreneurs and companies end up cheating and swindling lots of money. But earning money is always challenging; it is bound by ethics and the laws of nature.

People who have a making mindset will have a transactional attitude and a materialistic outlook. What we all know is all our savings are useless after our death. So why are we all after money? It is a crime if you have excess money in your bank account after your death. Giving is a blessing. It will provide you with lifelong joy. All earning mindset people are givers. (I've written about givers and takers in my title, Positive psychology)

At first, a person with a making mindset makes more money than a person with an earning mindset. But in the long run, only people who have an earning mindset can survive and achieve success. A person with an earning mindset will try to earn everything. These are the hard workers and doers in our society. These people are more creative workers. Rather than settling for mediocrity, they commit to achieving excellence.

The "making mindset" is a belief that hard work is nothing. This is why they all invariably believe in luck. To find luck, we look for a shortcut in life. Luck is when we are in the right place at the right time. However, both are unknown to us. We only know we are lucky when it happens to us.

Are you the type who resists all changes and diversity? Then it is clear that you're the one who seeks comfort. Success comes to those who push themselves to their limits. Have you ever seen Red Bull company advertisements? You can never expect anything more from an advertisement than Red Bull. Their aggressive stunts made Red Bull a household name in America. In 2012, they made an advertisement saying that "Red Bull gives you wings." It was an attempt to freefall from space. This space jump broke three records, the first human to break the speed of sound in free-fall; it was the highest free-fall in history (39,000 meters), and the longest distance free-fall.

This marketing stunt cost them more than thirty million dollars, but overall sales increased by 13% to five billion dollars.

Commercial success is driven by perception. There are more than a thousand shoe brands available today. Why do a few companies like Nike, Adidas, and Puma dominate the market? It is not that they believe they are the best; it is because we, consumers, believe they are the best. We feel a sense of appreciation when we wear these brands on our feet.

Many other brands are just as good as these brands or even better than these brands with very low prices. However, we are hooked on these brands. They never failed to keep their commitment. They have maintained the highest possible standard in all that they do. They always deliver what they have promised. This is why they are the best and they are growing. Each of these companies has a clear reason why they make their shoes.

The world is designed not by copying the subjects taught in universities but by solving the problems in the real world. The subjects in universities hardly change every year, but real-life situations change every day. The world is not run by the design of an IITians or Stanford alum but by the customer's needs and behaviours. Those who can crack it will always win.

It is said that we receive what we repeatedly do. Einstein once said the compound effect is the eighth wonder of the world. This essentially means that if there were easy ways to achieve success, then everyone would be doing so right now. If success could be cracked, everyone would. No hacker can ever decode the formula of success. There is no copy-paste formula for success.

You must understand how to harness the power of innovative ideas. In 1951, Toyota introduced creative ideas and suggestions for quality improvement. It is possible that plenty of people had similar concepts back then, but nobody was quite ready to tap into the potential of those ideas. It requires action, experimentation, the trial-and-error method, and much effort. Typically, we are not willing to spend time on it because of the uncertainty. This effort to harness the power of an idea contributed significantly to Toyota's success. Success is yours if you are willing to harness the power of any idea from any source.

Until you do something out of the ordinary, you will always end up being just like most people around you.

Success: A Philosophy

Bill Gates started coding when he was thirteen and fell in love with the process. If his thoughts were ordinary, perhaps today, he would have become a good software engineer at Google, not the founder of one of the most successful companies in the world. But he moved one step further and built Microsoft. He utilized his skills to the fullest extent possible. In this way, we can also produce genuinely great things. Find a way to use your ordinary talent to build something extraordinary.

Competence is a necessary condition for any great achievement. When your skills surpass those of your peers, you gain significant value. To become competent, you need to have 360° knowledge. Let me tell you what I meant to be to have 360° Knowledge.

I once asked a general manager about his strength. He said he knew the manufacturing process better than any other worker on the shop floor. This ability makes you a productive worker, but nothing more. Instead of focusing on administrative issues, he was more concerned with production-related problems. He got involved in every production process and corrected every employee from morning until night. If there were issues with production, he said, everyone should report them to him. Literally, he was performing the duties of a worker and not those of a manager.

In the epic Mahabharata, there is a story about Abhimanyu, a great warrior. He was the son of Arjuna and Subhadra, the half-sister of Lord Krishna. Abhimanyu was born and raised in Dwarka, where his father, Arjuna, and Lord Krishna taught him everything he needed to know about the world around him.

Abhimanyu participated in the great war of Kurukshetra and was responsible for the deaths of several great warriors. On the thirteenth day of the war, Abhimanyu entered the Chakravyuha.

While still a fetus in his mother's womb, Abhimanyu acquires the knowledge to enter the Chakravyuha. The story goes like this. Lord Krishna was explaining to his sister the strategies for entering the Chakravyuha (a military formation created by the Guru Dhronacharya on the thirteenth day after the death of Bhishma Pitamaha. It is the arrangement of soldiers that keeps moving in the form of a chakra, a spinning wheel on the battlefield). Subhadra fell asleep as Lord Krishna was explaining, and unborn Abhimanyu could not hear the second half about how to escape the Chakravyuha.

When Abhimanyu entered the Chakravyuha, Karna, with the assistance and instruction of Dhronacharya, launched an arrow that destroyed his bow and chariot. The Kaurava army took this opportunity to assassinate Abhimanyu. He died because he only learned how to enter the Chakravyuha, not how to get out of it.

In my opinion, knowledge acts in a circular way. Being a circle, we need to go around it in its entirety. The knowledge of this magnitude is not like that of a river, lake, or well; rather, it is more like an ocean.

What we miss most in our lives is clarity. Clarity comes from our interests, not others' interests. You are hesitant to take on additional responsibilities since you do not know what to do with your full heart. If you ask James Cameron to make a science fiction film for you, he will do it—not once, but many times. In the same way, if you are asked to do some extra work, you will probably say no because you don't like the job and don't know what interests make you excited at work. v You are on the road to success when you work and enjoy doing it every time without getting bored and can make a living from that.

The secret ingredient to success is the right effort and the right timing. We never know when the right time will come. But we can always maximize our efforts to compromise the time factor. The right proportion in everything you do is the key to success. The right things come from experimenting, practicing, improving, learning, fixing, adding, and eliminating everything we do daily. When you can identify what you want and where you are now, that will motivate you to make the right effort.

Identify the right things for your company. Ask yourself questions like, "Why aren't our customers happy?"

"Why are our employees underperforming?"

"Why am I not delivering the change?"

"Is the money I'm making today worthwhile to invest in the future?"

"Will my company survive the next ten years?"

If you are struggling to answer these questions, you still haven't figured out the right thing for your company.

Success is a never-ending process, so it takes time. You don't think about it until you reach your final destination. For instance, you were selected for our national cricket team. When you believe you are greater than 1.3 billion people, your career is over, as the Indian cricketer Sreesanth experienced. You have come so far, but there are still miles to go in your life.

Do you still believe that achieving success in life is difficult? Then, on the following full moon day, look at the moon and remain a bit longer to enjoy its beauty. Now, remember the fact that fifty-three years ago, in 1969, we humans landed and walked on that surface. If your dream is big enough, you can make it come true.

If someone comes near your deathbed and asks you if you have any last wishes, and your answer is no, this is a sign of your ultimate victory over your life. You are going to heaven with a joyful mind. The ultimate form of success is when you have no more desires left.

For me, it is not enough just to work and make a livelihood; I believe we are here to experience life to its fullest extent. If we focus on bread and butter, we only care about surviving, not living.

FAILURE

I believe no matter what standards, systems, or conditions you work in; there is always a chance of failure. Attempting to list all the potential causes of failure would be impossible. Millions of businesses have gone out of business around the world because they failed. But there aren't many, and keeping that in your mind may help you avoid failure to some extent.

If we can conclude failure in one sentence, it would be like this. "Failure is the unconscious development of an untrained, unethical, immature, and uneducated mind. We can call it a failure if the efforts yield no results".

If you're not improving, do not assume that you are surviving. Survival itself carries a negative connotation. Attempts to survive usually fail.

The one word we never want to hear in our lives is "failure," not because it is scary, but because we have conditioned ourselves in this manner. We all write exams to succeed, we all start companies to make them unicorns, and we all attend interviews to be chosen. To find out where the weakness is, we need to experience failure. For introspection, there are no other means available to us than failure. The more errors we commit, the more educated we become about the process. This comprehension will ultimately result in our growth. Failure is not a predetermined outcome but rather the consequence of unforeseeable events.

Thomas Alva Edison made a total of ten thousand unsuccessful attempts to build the light bulb. Can you imagine working eighteen hours a day, experimenting with more than 3000 theories, and failing 10,000 times, but each time becoming more determined to do the work? He once said, "I haven't failed in any of my efforts to manufacture a light bulb, but I have learned how not to build a light bulb in a thousand different ways." It was his attitude toward failure that made him the greatest of all time. If we can preserve this mindset in life, we will never fear failure.

"Take risks in life; if you win, you can lead; if you fail, you can guide," these are the golden words of swami Vivekananda. You don't need any other better explanation for failure. You will never be left behind if you fail; you can still guide others.

Failures are important stories to know. Not only do they help us realize what went wrong, but they also help us understand the patterns and results of each failure. Failure is never a prerequisite for success. This only proves that our efforts were for naught. Our destiny will be determined by what we've learned from every failure and how we've changed after each failure.

We usually think we have enough knowledge to handle any situation, even if we don't. The quickest way to get things done is to ask someone who knows the process very well. The process is just as important as a result. Learning from the mistakes of others is a great quality. This could preclude us from making the same mistakes again. We always work with people who don't know what to do, which makes things even worse.

When you are on an important mission, you should not focus on the result but on the process. A profound knowledge of the process is important. The process is what transforms black carbon into diamond, the most valuable material on earth. The process is what turns sand into gold. Because of the process, the sun provides us with energy 24/7. The process is the basis of every law and rule. The process drives our lives forward.

When the time comes to make important decisions and you have no deep knowledge of the process, you cannot deliver what you have promised.

If you do not wish to fail, measure what matters the most and measure what is unknown to you. You build your career based on what is known to you. But when you run a business, only measure what you need to know. We all make the same mistake; we always measure what we know and try to build our reputation on the knowledge we have. It doesn't matter how much you know; it matters how much you need to learn. It will only help you grow your ego, not lead you toward success.

"Vidhya Dhanam Sarvadhanal Pradhanam" is a famous ancient Sanskrit text. It conveys the notion that expertise is more crucial in the real world than anything else. Knowledge is relative and differs from person to person due to the impossibility of acquiring all relevant information. Our planet is estimated to be 4.5 billion years old. Nobody can fully comprehend four billion years of history in a single lifetime. Thus, knowledge is contextual and relative to a person's area of interest. Many of us are partially informed, which accelerates our chances of failure.

When we know ourselves well, it is easy to predict how strong or weak we are as a business. I'd like you to answer how likely your business go bankrupt in the next five years. If you can't answer, you haven't thought about the strengths, weaknesses, and risks involved in your business. When you know your threats, you'll be able to find areas to improve. Working on your strengths is more important than working on your weaknesses. When you know your strengths, you will take more calculated risks.

You must rethink your capabilities to thrive in the face of hardship and shifting consumer preferences. Today, change is inevitable, but before making any changes, ask these four questions: Why change? What is to change? How do I change? When should I change? If you can't give the right answers to these questions, you can't deal with the change.

Toyota is known for making high-quality cars. But what if they didn't come up with a new, energy-efficient, eco-friendly car? I don't think their legacy would help them. It's crucial to reframe your abilities in a way that fits in with what your customers are interested in. History shows us over and over again that if we don't rethink our strengths, we will lose our place in the market. Examples of such companies are Nokia, Kodak, General Motors, Compaq, Xerox, Polaroid, Motorola, and Blackberry, along with many other brands.

A sense of progress in everything you do is crucial for avoiding setbacks. Progress lies in exploration. Without failure, it is impossible to explore. Exploration is taking action without any bias. A person who believes the problem is more extensive than their life cannot do much to solve it. One who considers problems insignificant compared to life will succeed in solving many issues. Always look above the problem, not below or at its level, when tackling problems. If we do not rise above the situation, we will always blame others, find faults, ignore the problem, and not fix it at its root. What stands above the problem is not merely the ability to foresee its effects but rather the ability to eliminate them.

To explore the possibilities, you must be comfortable with both the known and the unknown. Consider yourself more of an innovator than a businessman. While a businessman looks at the bottom line, an innovator sees opportunities in everything. An innovative mindset will help you get back on your feet after every failure.

Problems and failures are intertwined. The more effectively you solve every problem, the less likely you fail. Failures offer us painful experiences. To avoid these unpleasant experiences, we avoid taking risks in our daily lives. The dread of committing errors is engrained inside us. Initially, we avoid facing problems so as not to fail. We leave the situation unchanged. Having such a mentality is the quickest route to failure.

You will not succeed if you start a business, but if you are committed to solving every problem and fulfilling your responsibilities as an entrepreneur, you will succeed.

Failures happen in the middle, and we presume they happened at the end. To move beyond every failure, we must improve 4C's, which are confidence, commitment, capability, and competence. V.G. Siddhartha, the founder and the CEO of Coffee Day, took his own life, which brought me great sorrow. As Indians, we should always be proud of the brands we established to compete in the global market. He may have overstated how bad his choices were and failed to convince himself. Possibly because of this, he took the crucial step.

Throw away all of your bad habits, because negative habits do not ensure life success, but positive habits do.

The world will remember only those who rise above success and failure. In other words, it is the state of being aware or pure consciousness. Success and failure are for common people like me.

You are suffering not only because you failed but also because you are emotionally attached to the outcome of the event. Failure is hard because it is something you don't want to go through. We must accept that a failure is an option, as there are no other choices.

Self-doubt is the greatest impediment to our personal development. Our greatest potential may be thwarted by our self-doubts. But it is quite natural and affects every one of us. Determine what is stopping us from realizing our full potential. Self-awareness and a shift in perspective are the only ways to overcome self-doubt. When it comes to developing one's self-confidence, affirmations should be performed often.

When we live like we are in a simulation and everything is controlled by another entity, then we are entitled to fail.

We cannot guarantee that our next space program will be a complete success. We cannot guarantee that the next antibiotic will be completely effective. We cannot guarantee that our next fighter jet engine will function flawlessly. We take failure as an option and continue forward. There is always a prospect of success if corrective actions are taken after every failure.

How to overcome a fear of failure? Make failure a part of your daily routine. Every day, do something that is very hard to do. The more you become acquainted with failure, the less it is going to bother you.

Submission

I know these titles are not something new for you. However, it is certain that one of these titles will reflect your current condition. For instance, if you have trouble controlling your anger, the title "emotional intelligence" is for you. If you have problems finding the right person for your company, then recruitment is the right title for you. If you have trouble solving problems, three ways of thinking are made for you.

During my research, I asked managers what their biggest challenges were. Virtually everyone responded they didn't know how to deal with their employees. They are unable to control costs, improve performance, boost efficiency, solve problems, generate new ideas, or motivate the team.

When employees are asked, they say they don't know how to organize their work or manage their time, they are afraid to work, there is no better way to communicate in the company, they can't learn anything, and so on.

Based on the inputs from my interviews, I compiled a 100-page report. I deduced the following nineteen titles based on these notes.

You will undoubtedly become the right person to work in a small business if you act on these titles.

www.ingramcontent.com/pod-product-compliance
Lightning Source LLC
LaVergne TN
LVHW061540070526
838199LV00077B/6858